DK EYEWITNESS

Summit Free Public Library

TOP
GOA

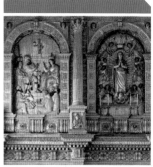

Top 10 Goa Highlights

The Top 10 of Everything

CONTENTS

Goa
Area by Area

Streetsmart

Within each Top 10 list in this book, no hierarchy
of quality or popularity is implied. All 10 are, in
the editor's opinion, of roughly equal merit.

Title page, front cover and spine *Palm-fringed
Palolem Beach*
Back cover, clockwise from top left *Anjuna
Flea Market; Anjuna Beach; Maruti Temple,
Panaji; Palolem Beach; Velha Goa*

**The information in this DK Eyewitness
Top 10 Travel Guide is checked regularly.**
Every effort has been made to ensure that
this book is as up-to-date as possible at the
time of going to press. Some details, however,
such as telephone numbers, opening hours,
prices, gallery hanging arrangements and
travel information are liable to change. The
publishers cannot accept responsibility for
any consequences arising from the use of
this book, nor for any material on third party
websites, and cannot guarantee that any
website address in this book will be a suitable
source of travel information. We value the
views and suggestions of our readers very
highly. Please write to: Publisher, DK Eyewitness
Travel Guides, Dorling Kindersley, 80 Strand,
London WC2R 0RL, Great Britain, or email
travelguides@dk.com

Welcome to
Goa

Idyllic beaches, sleepy fishing villages dotted with pretty white-washed churches, grand Indo-Portuguese mansions, mouthwatering coastal cuisine and lively nightlife heighten Goa's appeal as one of the country's most popular holiday destinations. Whether you're looking for a relaxed beach holiday or a cultural break, this enticing destination will offer you an experience, quite simply, like no other. With Eyewitness Top 10 Goa, it's yours to explore.

India's sunshine state has a distinct culture with ample evidence of the 400-odd years of Portuguese rule still apparent in the people's dress, language, cuisine and music. Its capital, **Panaji**, and **Central Goa** are at the historic and cultural heart, home to the Latin-influenced old quarter, **Fontainhas**, **Old Goa's** glorious Baroque churches, the exotic spice plantations of **Ponda**, **Molem's** wild nature reserves and the spectacular **Dudhsagar Falls**.

Goa's splendid beaches stretch over 105 km (65 miles), drawing around two million visitors every year. From Querim in the north to Mobor in the south, each beach has a distinct character. The continuous string of bustling **North Goa** beaches, including **Baga**, **Candolim**, **Calangute** and **Anjuna**, are packed with upscale resorts and have a bohemian vibe while the serene **South Goa** beaches offer a more relaxed atmosphere. A study in contrasts, Goa is simultaneously traditional and modern, noisy and serene.

Whether you're visiting for a weekend or a week, our Top 10 guide brings together the best of everything Goa has to offer, from palm-fringed golden beaches to a vibrant nightlife. The guide has useful tips throughout, from seeking out what's free to avoiding the crowds, plus six easy-to-follow itineraries, designed to tie together a clutch of sights in a short space of time. Add inspiring photography and detailed maps, and you've got the essential pocket-sized travel companion. **Enjoy the book, and enjoy Goa.**

Clockwise from top: **Palolem Beach, Church of St Francis of Assisi, colourful Goa Carnival float, paddy field in South Goa, Fort Aguada, Baga Beach shacks, spices at Anjuna Flea Market**

Exploring Goa

A favourite year-round holiday destination, Goa is packed with things to see and do. While it is tempting to find the perfect beach and just luxuriate there, the equally enticing hinterland offers an amazing variety of treasures to discover. Whether your visit is short or long, these itineraries will ensure that you experience the very best that Goa has to offer.

Tropical Spice Plantation grows a wide variety of spices and fruits. Spices have long been a principal export and an essential ingredient in Goa's fiery cuisine.

Two Days in Goa

Day ❶
MORNING
Begin with a heritage walk of **Panaji's** *(see pp20–23)* Latin Quarter, Fontainhas. Next, visit the Church of Our Lady of the Immaculate Conception, the city's most important landmark.
AFTERNOON
Explore the renowned **Basilica de Bom Jesus** *(see pp26–7)* in **Old Goa** *(see pp24–5)* before visiting the **Museum of Goa** *(see p13)* in Pilerne to admire the stunning collection of artworks. In the evening, head back to **Panaji** *(see pp20–23)* for a cruise along the Mandovi.

Day ❷
MORNING
Head to **Fort Aguada** *(see p12)*, set on a hilltop, to enjoy the superb views. Then take a break to relax at **Candolim Beach** *(see p12)*. Stop at **Bomra's** *(see p95)* for excellent Burmese cuisine.

Key
— Two-day itinerary
— Seven-day itinerary

AFTERNOON
Enjoy windsurfing or parasailing at **Calangute Beach** *(see p16)*. Wander through the bustling **Arpora Saturday Night Bazaar** *(see p93)*. You can try some Greek cuisine for dinner and enjoy views from **Thalassa** *(see p95)*.

Seven Days in Goa

Day ❶
Start the day early with a yoga session at **Ashvem** *(see p18)*. Drive to **Chapora Fort** *(see p14)* to enjoy the views from its ramparts. Follow this up with a dip in the fresh water spring at **Vagator** *(see p89)*.

Day ❷
At **Anjuna** *(see p15)* shop for souvenirs at the famous flea

Agonda Beach is famous as the nesting site for Olive Ridley turtles. Its calm waters make it a great spot to relax and unwind.

0 kilometres 15
0 miles 15

Tropical Spice Plantation
○ *Khandepar*
○ *Ponda*
○ *Molem*
Bhagwan Mahavir Wildlife Sanctuary ○
Dudhsagar Falls
○ *Braganza House*
Margao ○ *Palácio do Deão*
Salaulim Dam
gonda Beach
alolem
Silent Noise

market. Next, try your hand at a range of watersports at **Calangute Beach** *(see p16)*. Relax under a parasol on **Candolim Beach** *(see p12)*. Later, enjoy **Baga's** *(see p16)* legendary nightlife.

Day ❸
Visit some of the oldest churches in **Old Goa** *(see pp24–5)*, a UNESCO World Heritage Site. From here head to **Panaji** *(see pp20–23)* to explore the capital's oldest district, Fontainhas.

Day ❹
Head to **Ponda** *(see pp30–31)* to visit the many temples here. Next, take a tour of the Tropical Spice Plantation and enjoy a Goan buffet lunch. Then, head north to the village of Khandepar to admire the rock-cut caves, one of Goa's oldest historical monuments.

Day ❺
Set out early for the village of **Molem** *(see pp32–3)*, the main entry point to the Bhagwan Mahavir Wildlife Sanctuary. Explore the sanctuary before heading to Dudhsagar Falls for a swim.

Day ❻
Visit Goa's heritage city, **Margao** *(see pp34–5)*. Take a tour of the grandest colonial mansion in the state, Braganza House. Stop for a traditional meal at the Palácio do Deão. In the evening, head to Colva Beach for spectacular sunset views.

Day ❼
Start at quiet **Agonda Beach** *(see p38)*, a nesting site for the endangered Olive Ridley turtles. Next, head to Palolem for kayaking and stand-up paddleboarding. Then make your way to Silent Noise for a night of dancing.

Top 10 Goa Highlights

Fishermen on a wooden outrigger boat on Baga River

🔟 Goa Highlights

With its tropical setting and idyllic beaches, Goa needs little introduction. India's smallest state, has much more than sublime beaches. It is steeped in history and offers a multitude of cultural experiences, which is what makes it one of the most desirable tourist destinations.

① Candolim and Around

Upscale Candolim is great for watersports. Its white sands stretch all the way to the 17th-century Fort Aguada (see pp12–13).

Querim • Pernem • A
Arambol (Harmal)
Ashvem ④
Morjim • Siolim
Vagator & ② • Mapusa
Anjuna ③ Calangute &
Baga
Candolim ①
Panaji ⑤ ⑥
Dona Paula • Bamb
Vasco da
Gama • Dabolir
Bogmalo •

Arabian Sea

Benaulin
Var
Cavelos
B
Cabo da
Rama

② Vagator, Anjuna and Around

Dramatic hilltops and Chapora Fort provide Vagator Beach with a pretty backdrop. Adjacent Anjuna is famous for its flea market (see pp14–15).

③ Calangute and Baga

Goa's busiest beaches are home to countless shops, hotels, restaurants and nightclubs. The bustling Arpora Saturday Night Bazaar is a highlight (see pp16–17).

④ Ashvem and Around

The quietest stretch on Goa's north coast, Ashvem is popular for its yoga retreat centres and is perfect for watersport activities (see pp18–19).

⑤ Panaji

Portuguese colonial architecture, whitewashed churches, the pretty Latin-influenced old quarter along with authentic local cuisine are all found in Goa's relaxed capital, Panaji, overlooking the Mandovi (see pp20–23).

Old Goa ⑥

Once the Portuguese capital in India, glorious Old Goa still retains a number of beautiful Baroque churches as well as a magnificent cathedral and a basilica. These are considered to be among Goa's most significant monuments *(see pp24–7)*.

⑦ Ponda and Around

The town of Ponda is known for its numerous Hindu temples while its environs are home to exotic spice plantations *(see pp30–31)*.

Molem and Around ⑧

With plenty of forest trails and a variety of bird and plant species, Molem's lush nature reserves feature a wealth of attractions. It is also home to India's second highest waterfall, Dudhsagar *(see pp32–3)*.

⑨ Margao and Around

Scattered around South Goa's main market town Margao are many picturesque villages, which are home to stunning 18th- and 19th-century Indo-Portuguese mansions *(see pp34–7)*.

⑩ Palolem, Agonda and Around

Picture-postcard perfect Palolem is known for its sunset views. Neighbouring Agonda and Galgibaga are nesting sites of the Olive Ridley turtles *(see pp38–9)*.

TOP 10 ⭐ Candolim and Around

Once a sleepy fishing village in North Goa, Candolim derives its name from the Konkani word *kandoli* meaning dykes – a reference to the system of sluices used to reclaim the land from the nearby marshes. In 1787, it was at the centre of an attempt made to overthrow the Portuguese. Today, it is famous for its beach, Our Lady of Hope Church and nearby attractions such as Fort Aguada, Reis Magos and the Museum of Goa. A string of bars, restaurants and nightclubs line its main street and side lanes.

1 Fort Aguada

This fort **(above)** was built in 1612 as a defence against the Marathas and the Dutch. Its church is dedicated to St Lawrence, the patron saint of sailors. Some of the buildings in it once housed the state prison.

2 Candolim Beach

South of Calangute, this beach **(below)** stretches all the way to Fort Aguada. Popular with tour groups, the once peaceful waters *(see p89)* now resound with the whir of jet skis and speedboats.

3 Fort Aguada Lighthouses

In the centre of the fort is a four-storey lighthouse, erected in 1864, which is the oldest of its kind in Asia. The new lighthouse, built in 1976, is open to the public and offers great views from the top.

4 Reis Magos Church

Adjacent to the fort is the Reis Magos Church. Constructed in 1555, this is one of Goa's earliest churches, and has the royal Portuguese coat of arms on its façade.

Candolim and Around

5 Reis Magos Fort

The fort at Reis Magos was built in 1551 by Portuguese viceroy Don Alfonso de Noronha as a line of defence. It once housed a prison. Today, it is a cultural centre with a gallery showcasing Goan artist Mario Miranda's works and an exhibition detailing the history and restoration of the fort.

8 Our Lady of Hope Church

The bell towers of this unique church **(left)**, built in Mannerist Neo-Roman style, rise higher than the central gable. The church has a relic of the blessed Mother Teresa in the form of a drop of blood as well as her statue.

SUBODH KERKAR

Goan artist, Subodh Kerkar, has chronicled Goa's rich history through his work. At the Museum of Goa, look out for an old Goan fishing boat, adorned with antique Chinese soup spoons to highlight the history of the Chinese trade, while the huge chilli sculptures serve as a silent reminder of the old spice route.

10 Museum of Goa (MOG)

Founded by Subodh Kerkar, MOG (Konkani for love) features contemporary art by Indian and international artists. It also has an art store and café *(see p90)*.

6 Houses of Goa Museum

This boat-shaped building *(see p90)*, designed by architect Gerard da Cunha, showcases the history of Goan architecture. Displays are spread across levels interconnected by a spiral staircase.

7 Devil's Finger

This scenic spot, close to Fort Aguada, is the perfect place to enjoy stunning sunset views.

9 Sinquerim Beach

Extending up to the ramparts of Fort Aguada, Sinquerim Beach **(above)** has three luxury hotels on its sands. A few reliable operators offer a range of watersports facilities as well as boat trips.

NEED TO KNOW

Fort Aguada & Fort Aguada Lighthouses: MAP J6; Fort Aguada Rd, 0982 359 3995; open 9:30am–6pm daily

Candolim Beach: MAP H5

Reis Magos Church: MAP J6; Nerul–Reis Margos Rd; 0832 240 2370; open 6am–11pm daily

Reis Magos Fort: MAP J6; Verem; open 9:30am–5pm Tue–Sun; www.reismagos fort.com

Houses of Goa Museum: MAP K5; H. No. 674, Torda; 0832 241 0711; adm

Devil's Finger: MAP J6

Our Lady of Hope Church: MAP J5; Candolim; 0832 248 9084; open daily

Museum of Goa (MOG): MAP J5; Plot No 79, Pilerne Industrial Estate, Pilerne; open 10am–6pm daily; adm; www.museum ofgoa.com

Sinquerim Beach: MAP H6

■ The Aguada Hill Cycling Tour departs just below Nerul Bridge at 4:30pm every day.

TOP 10 ⭐ Vagator, Anjuna and Around

A beautiful bay sheltered by rocky outcrops at both ends, Vagator consists of small beaches fringed by shady coconut palms. It is the perfect place to discover Goa's unspoilt beauty. Looming above it are the red laterite ruins of Chapora Fort. Neighbouring Anjuna, known for its sprawling weekly flea market, has been a popular destination since the 1960s. Nearby are the pretty villages of Assagao, Siolim and North Goa's largest town, Mapusa.

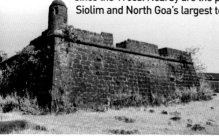

3 Fresh Water Springs

There are two fresh water springs in Vagator. One is close to Big Vagator, while the other is located at the southernmost cove of Ozran, which lies below a steep cliff.

YOGA RETREATS IN NORTH GOA

Goa is the perfect place to immerse yourself in a yoga retreat. Inland from Anjuna, Assagao is the heartland of yoga with numerous retreats (see p92). Some of them even run training programmes for teachers. The Himalaya Yoga Valley, the Satsanga Retreat and the Purple Valley Centre are among the most popular ones in North Goa.

1 Chapora Fort

Now in ruins, this fort **(above)** was built by the Portuguese in 1717 on the remains of a bastion erected by Adil Shah. Its name is derived from "Shahpura", or "Town of the Shah", as the village was once known. The ramparts offer great coast views.

Vagator, Anjuna and Around

2 Vagator Beach

Scenic Vagator's main beach (see p46) is known as Big Vagator **(below)**. To the south is secluded Little (or Ozran) Vagator where the main attraction is the face of Lord Shiva, carved out of the rocks.

4 Anjuna Beach

With its calm waters and palm trees, Anjuna *(see p47)* is one of the most scenic beaches of North Goa. A haven for backpackers, it is known for its rave parties.

5 Anjuna Flea Market

This popular Wednesday flea market **(below)** sells everything from Balinese batik and papier-mâché boxes to Tibetan prayer wheels and handmade leather sandals.

7 Mascarenhas Mansion

Built in the 16th century, this mansion in Assagao has beautiful *balcãos* (balconies) and stained-glass windows with floral designs. On the front porch there is an L-shaped wooden seat.

8 Mapusa

The highlight here is the lively Friday market *(see p63)*, with its tantalizing aromas of dried fish, spices and the spicy Goan sausages, *chouriço*. In demand are the region's famous cashew nuts.

10 Siolim

Set amid pretty verdant surroundings, the riverside village of Siolim *(see p91)* features striking colonial-era houses and the Church of St Anthony **(above)**, believed to be the site of two miracles in the 16th-century.

6 Assagao

Close to Anjuna lies Assagao *(see pp90–91)*, home to grand mansions and churches. Visitors can explore the area by taking a walk around the tranquil village.

9 Blue Whale Water Park

This water park at Arpora has a range of rides. Kids will love the "Finding Nemo Jumping Castle". There are four swimming pools here as well.

NEED TO KNOW

Chapora Fort: **MAP H3**; Chapora Fort Rd, Chapora; 0832 249 4200

Vagator Beach & Anjuna Beach: **MAP H4**

Anjuna Flea Market: **MAP H4**; Anjuna Beach; open Nov–Apr: 8am–sunset Wed

Assagao: **MAP J4**

Mascarenhas Mansion: **MAP J4**; Assagao

Mapusa: **MAP J4**; open 8am–6:30pm daily

Blue Whale Water Park: **MAP H4**; Baga–Arpora Rd, Arpora; 0777 404 9521; adm

Siolim: **MAP J3**

....

▪ Take the Assagao Heritage Walk *(0750 757 9072)* to learn about the history of the village.

▪ The Assagao Mehfil *(www.assagaomehfil. com)* hosts regular music concerts and dance performances.

▪ Enjoy a bird watching tour with Rahul Alvarez *(www.rahulalvares.com)*.

TOP 10 ⭐ Calangute and Baga

The centre of the hippie scene in the 1960s and 1970s, Calangute is Goa's most crowded beach. During the day, it is packed with sunbathers, trinket stalls and hawkers. The entire stretch of sand is lined with bars and restaurant beach shacks that serve Goan food. En route to the neighbouring picturesque village of Saligao is the colonial Casa dos Proença mansion and the churches of Mae de Deus and St Alex. Extending north of Calangute, Baga Beach is far less crowded, although its expanse of soft, white sand has its share of guesthouses and late-night clubs and bars along Tito's Lane.

Baga Beach ①

Next to Calangute, Baga **(right)** is Goa's most developed beach (see p47). It is dotted with several shacks, trendy eateries and lively night spots. Many operators here offer a wide range of watersport activities.

NEED TO KNOW

Baga Beach & Calangute Beach: MAP H5

Mario Gallery: MAP H5; Pedru Martina, Calangute; 0744 736 5372

Mae de Deus Church: MAP J5; Chogm Rd, Saligao; 0832 227 8246; open 9am–5pm daily

Tito's Statue: MAP H5

Tibetan Market: MAP H5; Calangute– Baga Rd, Baga; open 11am–11pm daily

St Alex Church: MAP J5; near Don Bosco School, Bardez; 0982 359 3995; open 9am–8:30pm daily

Casino Palms: MAP H4; 614, Calangute–Baga Rd, Baga; 0779 898 5000

Casa dos Proença: MAP H5; Calangute– Baga Rd

Literati: MAP H5; E/1-282 Gaura Vaddo, Calangute; 0832 227 7740

② Calangute Beach

Once regarded as the "queen of beaches", this is Goa's busiest beach (see p46). There's plenty for visitors to explore here including the market town, which has several Kashmiri-run handicraft boutiques and Tibetan stalls selling crafts and miniature paintings.

③ Mario Gallery

Legendary artist Mario Miranda's (1926–2011) original artworks are on display here. Large and small-size prints of his illustrations and merchandise can be purchased from the store. Miranda was famous for his sketches and cartoons of local characters and Goan culture.

④ Mae de Deus Church

This church **(below)** in Saligao is one of the best examples of Neo-Gothic architecture in Goa. Near the altar is the miraculous statue of Mae de Deus (Mother of God). The church looks stunning when it is illuminated in the evening.

6 Tito's Statue

In 1971, Tito Henry de Souza opened a small eatery to promote tourism in Goa. Today, Club Tito's (see p56) is a Goan institution. A life-size statue of Tito (left) is located in Baga.

7 Tibetan Market

This market has handcrafted jewellery, clothing and display pieces from Nepal and Tibet. Though expensive, the objets d'art leave no room for doubt as to their authenticity.

Calangute and Baga

5 St Alex Church

One of the oldest churches in Goa, St Alex's striking façade is dominated by a dome, flanked on each side by bell towers – one has a church bell while the other has a statue of Our Lady. The Rococo-style interior has an ornate pulpit and gilded reredos.

ARPORA SATURDAY NIGHT BAZAAR

Between the beaches of Baga and Anjuna is the vibrant and unmissable Arpora Saturday Night Bazaar (see p93). The market, spread over a vast area, begins at 7pm and has over 500 stalls selling everything from clothes, jewellery, and accessories to film posters and spices. Visitors can also sample drinks and mouthwatering food from the stalls, while enjoying the live music performances.

8 Casino Palms

The luxury spa and resort of La Calypso in Baga is home to the Casino Palms. There are many gaming tables for blackjack, roulette, mini-flush and baccarat. Several poker and slot machines are also available.

9 Casa dos Proença

This grand 18th-century mansion has a distinctive tower-shaped verandah with oyster-shell screens and a unique natural cooling system.

10 Literati

Set in a 100-year-old Portuguese house, Literati (below) has a great collection of books. It hosts literary and cultural events. Visitors can enjoy reading in the Italian-style garden café.

🔟⭐ Ashvem and Around

The pristine beaches to the far north of Goa are some of the region's loveliest and are a popular option for many travellers. Yoga, meditation and watersports are ubiquitous here. The beaches of Mandrem and Morjim are perfect for leisurely dips in the ocean. At sunset Ashvem comes alive attracting crowds to its bustling nightlife. Eclectic Arambol (or Harmal), a hippie haven in the 1960s, still retains some of its bohemian vibe.

Ashvem Beach ①

Even though the golden white sands of Ashvem **(right)** are getting crowded with each passing year, its seemingly never-ending shores *(see p47)* still remain the best place to relax under an umbrella.

② Mandrem Beach

The clear blue waters of Mandrem *(see p47)* and its pristine beach offer a peaceful respite from the packed beaches of the north.

④ Vaayu Waterman's Village

On the Ashvem–Mandrem beach road, this activity and art centre offers a wide range of watersports such as surfing, stand up paddle boarding and kayaking **(below)**.

⑤ Arambol Beach

Popular Arambol *(see p47)* still has all the charm of a traditional fishing village. Surrounded by low cliffs and featuring several dramatic rocky outcrops that jut into the sea, its calm waters are safe for swimming.

③ Ashiyana Yoga Centre

Set amid tropical gardens **(above)**, this retreat on the banks of the Mandrem River has five yoga *shalas* (studios). It offers world-class yoga classes with accommodation in treehouses and wooden eco-lodges.

⑧ Paliem Sweet Water Lake

At the northern end of Arambol, a rocky footpath leads to a second beach, Paliem, entirely surrounded by cliffs. This sandy cove has a freshwater lagoon **(above)** fed by hot springs and lined with sulphurous mud.

ARAMBOL DRUM CIRCLE

At the far end of Arambol Beach is sunset point, a popular spot in the evenings when a group of musicians gather in a circle to play various instruments, including the drums. The tribal beats of the drum circle inspire holiday-makers on the beach to join the crowds and dance to the rhythm of the drums.

⑨ Querim Beach

A 5-km- (3-mile-) long path, heading north from Arambol, leads to the quiet Querim Beach (pronounced "keri"). This pristine strip of white sand (see p47) is the perfect place to unwind or simply enjoy a leisurely swim.

⑩ Kitesurfing, Mandrem

The calm waters of Mandrem are safe for learning kitesurfing. Due to the wind patterns, the kiting season usually begins only in January. Several schools offer beginner and advanced level courses.

Ashvem and Around

[map with labels: Tiracol, ⑨, Querim, Paliem, Arambol, ⑤, ⑧ ⑥, ②, Mandrem, ⑦, ⑩, ③, Ashvem, Morjim, Siolim, Vagator, ④ ①]

⑥ Paragliding, Arambol

The cliffside near Paliem Sweet Water Lake is a good vantage point for paragliding. For details, check with Arambol Hammocks or the Western India Paragliding Association shack, which is close to the lake.

⑦ Sunset Beach Market

This market on Arambol Beach begins just a little before sunset. It sells handmade jewellery and quirky trinkets. Visitors are also treated to juggling acts and other stunts by performers here.

NEED TO KNOW

Ashvem Beach: **MAP G3**

Mandrem Beach: **MAP G2**

Ashiyana Yoga Centre: **MAP G2**; Junas Waddo, Mandrem; 0985 040 1714; open 8am–8pm daily

Vaayu Waterman's Village: **MAP H2**; Ashvem Beach Rd, opp. Holy Cross Chapel, Ashvem; 0985 005 0403

Arambol Beach: **MAP G2**

Paragliding, Arambol: Arambol Hammocks;

0961 917 5722; www.arambol.com

Sunset Beach Market & Paliem Sweet Water Lake: **MAP G2**

Querim Beach: **MAP G1**

Kitesurfing, Mandrem: Kiteguru Kitesurf School: Riverside Hotel, Mandrem; 7030 972 954; open Nov–Mar; www.kiteguru.co.uk

■ **Vaayu Waterman's Village** has an art gallery and a restaurant.

TOP 10 ★ Panaji

Reminiscent of a provincial Mediterranean town, Goa's capital, Panaji is situated at the mouth of the Mandovi River. Formerly a port of the kings of Bijapur, it became a military landing stage after the arrival of the Portuguese in 1510. In 1843, Panaji, or Panjim as it was then called, became the official capital of Portuguese territories in India. Today, it has a relaxed and friendly ambience, notably along the leafy avenues of the old town.

Church of Our Lady of the Immaculate Conception ①

Panaji's most important landmark, this church (right), built in 1541, is where Portuguese sailors would come to pray after their long voyage from Lisbon. Its most striking feature is the double flight of stairs leading up to the church *(see p75)*.

② Fontainhas

The narrow winding streets of the city's Latin-influenced old quarter *(see p76)* is lined with colourful houses, reminiscent of the Portuguese legacy.

③ Statue of Abbé de Faria

This arresting statue (above) is a tribute to Goan priest, Abbé de Faria. Born in Candolim, he won acclaim as the father of modern hypnosis. He also finds mention in Alexander Dumas's famous novel, *The Count of Monte Cristo*.

⑤ Ashokan Pillar

In the centre of the Municipal Gardens stands the Ashokan Pillar. The pillar initially featured a bust of explorer Vasco da Gama, but this was later replaced with the Buddhist Wheel of Law or the Ashoka Chakra, India's national emblem.

RIVER CRUISES

A delightful way to spend an evening is to take a sunset cruise along the Mandovi River. Operators also organize specialized tours through the backwaters, a vibrant mangrove habitat that is home to crocodiles. Tours by Pascoal Spice Farm *(see p84)* take visitors to the sylvan settings of spice plantations, which attract flocks of birds.

④ Gallery Gitanjali

Housed in a heritage complex, this gallery (below) is an art and cultural hub. Abstract art is on display here and in Panjim People's, Panjim Inn and Panjim Pousada hotels, which are part of the complex.

Panaji

Mandovi River

DAYANAND BANDODKAR MARG

MAHATMA GANDHI ROAD

FONTAINHAS

ALTINHO HILL

MALA

8 Institute Menezes Braganza

The *azulejos* (blue-and-white painted ceramic tiles) here are the highlight. These depict scenes from the epic *Os Lusiadas*, which recounts the history of the Portuguese presence in Goa.

9 Palace of Maquinezes

A great example of Goan period architecture, this building belonged to Portuguese land-owners called Maquinezes.

6 Church Square

At the heart of Panaji is a leafy park known as Church Square or the Municipal Gardens, originally named after 16th-century physician, Jardim de Garcia da Orta.

7 Altinho Hill

On the eastern edge of Panaji is the hill-top residential district of Altinho, which is home to the Bishop's Palace. The pope stayed at the palace during his visit in 1999.

NEED TO KNOW

Church of Our Lady of the Immaculate Conception: **MAP L2**; Rua Emidio Garcia; open 9am–7:30pm daily

Fontainhas: **MAP L2–M2**

Statue of Abbé de Faria: **MAP L1**

Gallery Gitanjali: **MAP M2**; E-212, 31st January Rd, Fontainhas; 0832 242 3331; open 9am–6pm daily

Ashokan Pillar: **MAP L1**

Church Square: **MAP L1**

Altinho Hill: **MAP L2**; Bishop's Palace: open 9am–5pm Mon–Fri (to 1pm Sat)

Institute Menezes Braganza: **MAP L1**; 0832 222 4143; open 10am–5:30pm Mon–Sat

Palace of Maquinezes: **MAP K1**; Dayanand Bandodkar Marg, Old GMC Complex; 0832 242 8111

Campal Gardens: **MAP K1**

10 Campal Gardens

These pleasant riverside gardens **(above)** are a good place to unwind. Visitors can also enjoy paddleboat rides on the Mandovi. Look out for a huge statue of Bhagwan Mahavir (the 24th Jain Tirthankara) here.

Exploring Panaji

Picturesque setting of Cabo Raj Niwas, the oldest residence in the country

1 Cabo Raj Niwas
MAP C3 ■ Raj Bhavan Rd, Dona Paula ■ 0832 245 3506

Constructed in 1540, this fortress (see p76) is the official residence of the Governor of Goa. The 500-year-old chapel is open to the public.

2 Azad Maidan
MAP L1 ■ MG Rd, near Police Headquarters, Ozari

This grassy square has a pavilion, made using Corinthian pillars taken from a Dominican church. Inside is a memorial to freedom fighter, Dr Tristao de Braganza Cunha.

3 St Sebastian's Chapel
MAP M2 ■ St Sebastian Rd, Altinho

The chapel has a life-size unusual crucifix, which shows Christ with his eyes open. It is believed this was done to inspire fear in those being interrogated during the Inquisition.

4 Old Secretariat
MAP L1 ■ Ave Dom João Castro

This riverfront edifice is one of Panaji's oldest buildings. Originally the summer palace of 16th-century ruler, Yusuf Adil Shah, it was later converted by the Portuguese as a residence for the viceroy. Today, it houses municipal offices and is one of the main venues for the annual Serendipity Arts Festival (see p69).

Colonial façade of the Old Secretariat

5 Casa da Moeda
MAP M1 ■ Near Head Post Office ■ www.casadamoedagoa. wordpress.com

In the midst of Panaji's Post Office Square stands the Casa da Moeda (House of Coins). This building served as the Mint of Goa from 1834 to 1841. Guests can enjoy afternoon tea here and learn more about the local history, but before visiting a booking needs to be made at least 48 hours in advance.

Exploring Panaji

6 Public Astronomical Observatory (PAO)

MAP L2 ▪ Junta House, Swami Vivekanand Rd ▪ 0832 222 5726

Located on the terrace of the Junta building, the PAO is the perfect place for astronomy enthusiasts and for those who would like to enjoy great night views of the capital city.

7 Kala Academy

MAP K2 ▪ Dayanand Bandodkar Marg ▪ 0832 242 0452

On the banks of the Mandovi is Goa's main cultural centre, which hosts performing arts events all year round. Built by architect Charles Correa, the complex has an indoor and open-air auditorium, a black box theatre, an art gallery and an on-site café.

8 Pilar Museum

MAP C3 ▪ 12 km (7 miles) SE of Panaji ▪ 0832 221 8521

Set on a hilltop, Pilar Seminary was originally built by the Capuchins (a Franciscan order) in 1613, on the site of an old Hindu temple. It has a small museum, which displays Portuguese coins and a stone lion, the symbol of the Kadamba dynasty.

Roger Ballen's show at Sunaparanta

9 Sunaparanta, Goa Centre for the Arts

MAP L2 ▪ 63/C-8, near Army House, Altinho ▪ www.sgcfa.org

Housed in a pretty villa, Sunaparanta (Konkani for Golden Goa) is a non-profit arts foundation set up by Dipti and Dattaraj Salgaocar. Under honorary director Siddharth Dhanvant Shanghvi's watch, the centre hosts various events, including the Sensorium festival *(see p69)*.

10 Panaji Riverfront

MAP M1

Enjoy a riverside stroll from Avenida Dom João de Castro to Campal, passing by the Old Secretariat and Campal Gardens *(see p21)*.

FONTAINHAS AND SÃO TOMÉ

Tucked away between Ourem Creek and Altinho Hill in Panaji are the old residential quarters of Fontainhas and São Tomé, built on reclaimed land in the 19th century. Fontainhas was named after the fountain of Phoenix, a spring that was the quarter's only source of water. Most of the houses are painted yellow, ochre, green or indigo in keeping with the traditional Portuguese building code that every building, except churches, should be

colour-washed after the monsoons. São Tomé takes its name from the tiny church, built in 1849. This old-world precinct, characterized by a jumble of painted, tile-roofed houses, has streets lined with taverns offering Goan cuisine and *feni* (cashew nut liqueur), and bakeries serving *bebinca*, the delicious local cake.

Rua de Ourem facing Ourem Creek

TOP 10 ⭐ Old Goa

A magnificent complex of churches spread along a 1.5-km (1-mile) stretch marks the site of Old Goa, the Portuguese capital until the mid-18th century. Portugal's Goa Dourada ("Golden Goa") was once a city inhabited by more than 30,000 people. The area, now a UNESCO World Heritage Site, has two of the state's most important religious monuments, the Basilica de Bom Jesus and the grand Sé Cathedral.

5 Archaeological Museum

Housed in the Convent of St Francis of Assisi, this museum **(below)** exhibits pre-colonial sculptures. A statue of the Portuguese general, Alfonso de Albuquerque, who conquered Goa in 1510, stands near the museum entrance.

1 Viceroy's Arch

Over 1,000 ships a year brought new arrivals to Goa in the 17th century. They passed under this archway **(above)**, built by Francisco da Gama (Viceroy, 1597–1600).

2 Basilica de Bom Jesus

The basilica (see pp26–7) was the first in South Asia to be granted the status of Minor Basilica in 1946. It is revered by Roman Catholics since it houses the mortal remains of Goa's patron saint, Francis Xavier.

3 Church of St Francis of Assisi

This is one of Old Goa's most important churches (see p45). Built by the Franciscan friars in 1521, it has a carved and gilded main altar, which depicts the crucified Jesus, four Evangelists, St Francis, and Our Lady with the infant Jesus.

4 Church and Monastery of St Augustine

Erected by the Augustinian order in 1597, this Gothic-style church (see p44) was abandoned in 1835, and its roof caved in seven years later. The belfry **(below)** is all that remains of what was once India's largest church.

7 Church of Our Lady of the Rosary

This is one of Goa's earliest Manueline-style churches. The tomb of Dona Catarina, the first Portuguese woman to migrate to Goa, lies here.

8 Gateway of Adil Shah's Palace

The gate, comprising a lintel and basalt pillars, is all that survives of Yusuf Adil Shah's palace. It was also used as the viceroys' residence until 1695.

THE ARCHITECTURE OF OLD GOA

Most of the buildings encompass a range of European styles, from sober Renaissance to exuberant Baroque and Portuguese Manueline, named after its patron King Manuel I, which uses nautical motifs. Almost all the churches are made of local laterite, a red and porous stone traditionally coated with lime whitewash to prevent erosion during the monsoons.

6 Church of St Cajetan

Built by Italian friars, this church **(above)** is known for the exuberant wood-carvings on its high altar and pulpit. The dome is laid out in the shape of a Greek cross *(see p44)*.

Old Goa

[Map showing locations 1–10 along the Mandovi River, NH4A, Gandhi Circle, Old Goa Rd, and Belgaum-Panaji Highway]

9 Church of Our Lady of the Mount

Goa's first viceroy, Alfonso de Albuquerque, built this church in 1526 after his victory over Yusuf Adil Shah. The church sits on top of a hill and offers great views of Old Goa.

10 Sé Cathedral

Designed in the 16th century and built over a period of 80 years, this cathedral *(see p75)* is believed to be Asia's largest. The gilded high altar depicts the life of St Catherine of Alexandria on six panels.

NEED TO KNOW

Viceroy's Arch: **MAP M6**

Basilica de Bom Jesus: **MAP M6**; Rua das Naus de Ormuz; 0832 228 5790; open daily

Church of St Francis of Assisi: **MAP M6**; Off NH 4; open 7:30am–6:30pm daily

Church and Monastery of St Augustine: **MAP M6**

Archaeological Museum: **MAP M6**; Convent of St Francis of Assisi;

0832 228 5333; open 9am–5pm Sat–Wed

Church of St Catejan: **MAP M6**; E of Viceroy's Arch; open daily

Church of Our Lady of the Rosary: **MAP M6**

Gateway of Adil Shah's Palace: **MAP M6**

Church of Our Lady of the Mount: **MAP M6**

Sé Cathedral: **MAP M6**; Senate Square; open 7am–6:30pm daily

Basilica de Bom Jesus

Imposing façade of Basilica de Bom Jesus

is mounted on a plinth. At the base are bronze plaques depicting scenes from his life.

4 Reredos
One of the highlights is the massive ornate gilded *reredos* (ornamental screen), which extends from floor to ceiling behind the altar. It features spiralling scrollwork, exquisitely carved panels, statues and pilasters.

1 Façade
This is the only Goan church not covered in lime plaster. The Baroque structure blends Doric, Corinthian, Ionic and composite styles in its three-tiered façade. At the top on a quadrangular pediment is an intricately carved basalt stone tablet, which features the Jesuit motto, IHS or *Iaeus Hominum Salvator*, meaning "Jesus the Saviour" in Greek.

2 Chapel of St Francis Xavier
Inside the basilica is a chapel where the relics of St Francis Xavier are kept. The interior of this chapel has paintings, depicting scenes from the life of the saint.

3 Tomb of St Francis Xavier
The marble-and-jasper three-tiered tomb of St Francis Xavier features the altars, the Florentine mausoleum and the silver casket. In 1698, St Francis's body was moved here on the request of the Duke of Tuscany, Cosimo III, who donated the elaborate tomb in exchange for the pillow that lay under the saint's head. The silver casket containing the saint's body

5 Sacristy
Adjoining the Chapel of St Francis Xavier is a corridor, which leads to the sacristy, accessed by a beautifully carved wooden door. Inside is an altar, that has an iron chest containing the Golden Rose, gifted by Pope Pius XII in 1953.

6 Main Altar
The massive gilt altarpiece is dominated by a statue of St Ignatius of Loyola, founder of the Jesuit Order accompanied by the Infant Jesus (Bom Jesus). The saint is seen gazing above his head at the gilded

The magnificent main altar

sun, which bears the Jesuit emblem IHS. Above this is a depiction of the Holy Trinity.

7 Gallery of Modern Art

On the upper floor of the basilica is a church art gallery, which displays the works of Goan surrealist painter, Dom Martin. The paintings, which date from 1973 and 1976 depict various Biblical scenes.

8 Interior Courtyard

The courtyard inside has a small garden. From here a corridor leads visitors to the sound and light show, which tells the story of St Francis Xavier.

9 Professed House of the Jesuits

Next to the basilica is a two-storey laterite building, which predates the basilica, having been completed in 1585. The building was used as the priests' quarters until it was damaged by a fire in 1633.

10 Our Lady to Bernadette at Lourdes

Outside there is a grotto with a spring of water, which depicts the apparition of Our Lady to Bernadette at Lourdes.

Paintings at the Gallery of Modern Art

ST FRANCIS XAVIER (1506–1552)

Francis Xavier was sent to Goa by the Portuguese king, Dom Joao III. He arrived in May 1542, aged 36, and worked tirelessly as a missionary over the next few years. He died while on voyage off the coast of China in 1552, and was temporarily buried on an island. When his body was dug up three months later to transfer his bones, it showed no signs of decay. A year later, when his remains were enshrined in the basilica in Goa, his body was still in pristine condition. This was declared a miracle, and in 1622 he was canonized. Expositions of his relics take place every ten years or so; the next one will be in 2024.

Casket with the body of St Francis Xavier

Ponda and Around

A busy commercial centre, Ponda lends its name to the *taluka* (sub-district) of the same name, which is renowned for its 17th- and 18th-century Hindu temples, tucked away in thick forests and the Safa Shahouri Masjid. To the north of the town is a butterfly sanctuary, with over 100 species while to the northeast, near the village of Khandepar, is a cluster of rock-cut caves. In and around Ponda, there are many farms that grow numerous aromatic spices.

1 Naguesh Temple

Built for the worship of Nagesh (Shiva as Lord of the Serpents), this is one of the oldest temples **(above)** in the region. The entrance hall has carved wooden friezes depicting scenes from the epics *Ramayana* and *Mahabharata* (see p45).

SPICE PLANTATIONS

The temple town of Ponda is the centre of spice farms (see p55), known for growing aromatic spices such as cardamom, nutmeg, cinnamon and vanilla, in addition to crops such as cashew, betel nut and coconut. Visitors can learn how the spices are grown by taking a guided tour of the plantation. The tour usually involves a stroll through the orchards and includes a traditional banana-leaf buffet lunch.

---

2 St Roque Chapel

Located atop a hill in Bandoda village, this chapel was built in 1904. The bell, which hangs in the chapel, has inscriptions in Devanagari as well as Portuguese.

3 Tropical Spice Plantation

Visitors will need to cross a bamboo bridge to get to this spice farm **(right)**. Bird watchers will enjoy spotting different species when paddle boating around the lake. There's a butterfly garden here (see p84) too.

4 Savoi Spice Plantation

About 13 km (8 miles) north of Ponda, is the 200-year-old Savoi Spice Plantation. One of the oldest plantations in Goa, it is known for growing coconuts, betel nuts and spices. Visitors can opt for an overnight stay in any of the village-style huts available here.

Previous pages Aerial view of the lovely Reis Magos Church

5 Mahalasa Temple

Dedicated to Vishnu, the main deity here was taken from Verna, a village in Salcete. Highlights include a 21-tier brass pillar, rising from a figure of Kurma (Vishnu's incarnation as a turtle), with Garuda, (half man, half eagle) his vehicle, perched on top.

6 Safa Shahouri Masjid

This mosque **(above)** was built by Ibrahim Adil Shah (successor of Yusuf Adil Shah) in 1560. A ritual tank here *(see p84)* has the same designs as those on the *mihrabs* (arched niches) inside the mosque.

10 Ponda Fort

Destroyed by the Portuguese in 1549, this fort was rebuilt in 1675 when the 17th-century Maratha leader, Shivaji, conquered the region. Inside, there's a statue in honour of Shivaji.

7 Caves of Khandepar

Deep in the forest, there are four Hindu rock-cut caves **(right)** from the 10th–13th centuries, with carved lotus decorations on the ceiling, simple door frames and niches for oil lamps.

Ponda and Around

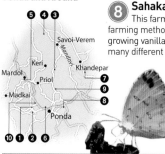

8 Sahakari Spice Farm

This farm is known for adopting organic farming methods for cultivation. It specializes in growing vanilla, spices, cashew nuts, fruits and many different ayurvedic medicinal herbs.

9 Butterfly Conservatory of Goa

Nature enthusiasts will enjoy a trip to this conservatory *(see p55)*, which is 5 km (3 miles) north of Ponda. Visitors can spot several species of butterflies **(left)** here.

NEED TO KNOW

Naguesh Temple: **MAP D3**; Donshiwado; open 6:30am–12:45pm, 4:30–8:30pm daily

St Roque Chapel: **MAP D3**; Donshiwado, Bandoda

Tropical Spice Plantation: **MAP D3**; Arla Bazar, Keri; 0832 234 0329; open 10am–4pm daily; adm

Savoi Spice Plantation: **MAP D3**; 50 Savoi, Marcel Ponda Rd; 0832 231 2394; open 9:30am–4:30pm daily; adm

Mahalasa Temple: **MAP D3**; Mahalasa Saunsthan, Mardol; open 6:30am–8:30pm Mon–Fri

Safa Shahouri Masjid: **MAP D3**; Shahpur Rd, Ponda; open 5am–9pm daily

Sahakari Spice Farm: **MAP D3**; Ponda Belgaum Highway, Curti; adm

Caves of Khandepar: **MAP D3**; Deulwada, Surla

Butterfly Conservatory of Goa: **MAP D3**; Priol; 9822 125 474; open 9:30am–4:30pm daily; adm

Ponda Fort: **MAP D3**; NH 4A, Donshiwado, Bandoda

Molem and Around

Close to the Karnataka border, the village of Molem is the starting point for a region of great natural beauty, abundant wildlife and sacred architectural gems. Bhagwan Mahavir Wildlife Sanctuary is one of the largest protected wildlife areas in Goa. In the southeast corner of the sanctuary is the famous Dudhsagar Falls. The medieval Tambdi Surla temple lies at the northern end, on the dense lower slopes of the Western Ghats.

1 Dudhsagar Falls

Goa's 600-m- (1,969-ft-) high waterfall **(right)** gets its name Dudhsagar (meaning "sea of milk" in Konkani) from the clouds of white mist that rise when the water level is at its highest. It is best visited after the monsoon from October until December (see p81).

2 Mahishasura Mardini Temple

Dedicated to goddess Navdurga, this temple is believed to be more than 500 years old. The main deity worshipped here is Mahishasura Mardini, a fierce incarnation of goddess Durga created to slay the buffalo-demon, Mahishasura.

3 Bhagwan Mahavir Wildlife Sanctuary and Molem National Park

One of Goa's most interesting nature reserves, Bhagwan Mahavir Wildlife Sanctuary covers a vast area of 240 sq km (93 sq miles) that also includes Molem National Park. It is home to jungle cats, deer, leopards **(left)** and *gaurs* (Indian bison) and over 120 bird species. There are several unmarked forest trails here. Guided tours of the park are available.

4 Backwoods Camp

Nature lovers will enjoy a trip to this camp, near Tambdi Surla, which is home to over 170 species of endemic and migratory birds, from the pretty Ceylon frogmouths and Asian fairy bluebirds to the Malabar trogon and Indian pitta. Farmhouse rooms, bungalows and tents are available for stay here.

5 Tambdi Surla Mahadev Temple

This is the oldest existing Hindu temple **(above)** in Goa from the Kadamba period. Dedicated to Shiva, the temple *(see p82)* is built from black basalt and probably survived because of its remote location.

6 Sunset Point

A picturesque spot, which offers lovely views of the tropical evergreen forest. Visitors can hire a four-wheel-drive vehicle at the Molem check-point to reach here.

Molem and Around

NEED TO KNOW

Dudhsagar Falls: **MAP F4**; open 6:30am–5:00pm daily; adm (additional charge for photography)

Mahishasura Mardini Temple: **MAP E4**; Cormonem

Bhagwan Mahavir Wildlife Sanctuary: **MAP F4**; 0832 222 1505; open 7am–5pm daily; adm

Backwoods Camp: **MAP F3**; 0942 007 2007

Tambdi Surla Mahadev Temple, Sunset Point, Tambdi Surla Waterfall & Nature Interpretation Centre: **MAP F3**

Jungle Book Resort: **MAP F3**; 0982 212 1441

Devil's Canyon: **MAP F4**

■ Tickets to the wildlife sanctuary are available at the Nature Interpretation Centre.

■ Devil's Canyon may be closed at the end of the monsoons when the water levels are high.

GETTING TO DUDHSAGAR FALLS

The best way to get to the falls is via the village of Colem *(see p83)*, about 7 km (4 miles) south of Molem, by car or by local train from Margao. At Colem, rent a shared jeep and be ready for the bumpy 45-minute journey to the falls. The jeeps available for hire wait at the drop-off point before bringing visitors back to Colem. Another option is the full-day Goa Tourism "Dudhsagar Special" tour, from Calangute and Panaji.

9 Jungle Book Resort

In the small village of Colem (Kulem), this resort offers activities ranging from jungle trekking to ziplining **(below)**. Visitors can stay overnight in the simple mud huts here.

7 Tambdi Surla Waterfall

Almost as high as Dudhsagar, this waterfall is 2 km (1.2 miles) north-west of Tambdi Surla. Adventure enthusiasts will enjoy trekking through the dense foliage and steep rocky trail, with the help of experienced guides to get to the base of this waterfall.

8 Nature Interpretation Centre

Located within the sanctuary, this centre provides information on the diverse array of plant and animal life to help visitors understand and learn more about the native flora and fauna that can be seen here.

10 Devil's Canyon

This scenic river gorge in the sanctuary consists of a zig-zagging mass of rock with underground passages. Visitors should be careful not to swim here as the undercurrents are quite strong and treacherous.

TOP 10 ⭐ Margao and Around

Goa's second most important city after Panaji, Margao (Madgaon) is the administrative and commercial capital of the South Goa district. Located nearby is Colva, one of the most developed beach resorts in South Goa. Inland from Margao, the villages of Loutolim and Chandor are home to several beautiful colonial *palacios*. Further east lies the small hamlet of Rachol, which originally was the site of an old fortress built by the Bijapur sultans.

1 Church of the Holy Spirit

This towering Baroque church **(below)** has a grand interior with an impressive stucco ceiling, a gilded pulpit, Rococo altar and elegant altarpieces in the transepts.

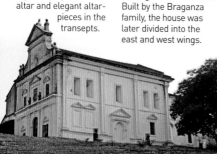

4 Braganza House

The impressive scale of Braganza House *(see pp36–7)*, and its magnificent interior, make it Goa's grandest mansion. Built by the Braganza family, the house was later divided into the east and west wings.

6 Rachol Seminary

Spectacularly located on the summit of a hill, this seminary **(above)** has a fort-like façade, flanked by watchtowers. Adjacent to it is the Church of St Ignatius Loyola, dedicated to the eponymous saint. According to legend, bone fragments and a vial of his blood are enshrined near the entrance.

2 Monte Hill

East of the church, a road winds up to Monte Hill. Although visitors cannot enter the chapel at the top of the hill, the views across Margao's rooftops of the southern coast from here are great.

5 Goa Chitra Museum

This ethnographic museum **(below)** is set on a working organic farm. It aims to promote the region's traditional agrarian lifestyle and has antique agricultural tools and artifacts on display.

3 Figueiredo Mansion

Believed to be more than 500 years old, this mansion *(see p100)* has a narrow passage with disguised gun holes, below the building. The Figueiredo family used this as an escape tunnel when attacked by bandits.

Margao and Around

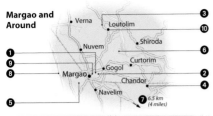

GOA'S COLONIAL MANSIONS

Villages around Margao have colonial country mansions, dating from the 18th to the 19th centuries, when local landlords began to profit from Portugal's control over the maritime trade routes from Africa to Malaysia. Loutolim nearby was an important Portuguese administrative centre, and has many stately homes. South of Margao, Chinchinim and Benaulim also have fine mansions.

10 Ancestral Goa

This model village (see p100) depicts Goan life from a bygone era. Here there are statues of tradesmen, miniature colonial homes as well as a laterite sculpture **(below)** of Mirabai (see p55).

7 Palácio do Deão

Built as a country house by Portuguese nobleman Jose Paulo de Almeida, this colonial mansion (see p100) with its tropical gardens was once a retreat for the colony's viceroys. Visitors can enjoy lunch on the terrace, overlooking the Kushavati River.

8 Colva Beach

One of Goa's longest stretch of sand, Colva's (see p98) proximity to Margao makes it an ideal summer retreat. It is dotted with seafood cafés.

9 Sat Burnzam Ghor

Named after the original seven gables on its roof, this mansion is Goa's only surviving example of a house with a pyramidal roof.

NEED TO KNOW

Church of the Holy Spirit: **MAP B5**; Holy Spirit Rd, Borda; 0832 271 4005; open 9am–noon, 4–7pm daily

Figueiredo Mansion: **MAP B4**; Loutolim; 0832 277 7028; open 9am–5pm daily; adm; www.figueiredo house.com

Braganza House: **MAP C6**; Chandor; 0832 278 4201; open 9am–6pm daily; adm

Goa Chitra Museum: **MAP B5**; Benaulim; 0832 657 0877; open 9am–6pm daily; adm; www.goachitra.com

Rachol Seminary: **MAP C5**; 0832 277 6052; www.racholseminarygoa.org

Palácio do Deão: **MAP E4**; Quepem; 0832 266 4029; open 10am–5pm Sat–Thu; www.palaciododeao.com

Colva Beach: **MAP D4**

Sat Burnzam Ghor: **MAP B5**; 0832 266 4029

Ancestral Goa: **MAP B4**; Loutolim; 0832 227 7034; open 9am–6pm daily; adm; www.ancestralgoa.com

Braganza House

1 East and West Wing
The mansion is divided into two separate wings, occupied by different branches of the Braganza family. The descendants of Antonio Elzario Sant'Anna Pereira occupy the east wing, while the Menezes Braganzas live in the west wing.

2 Hallway
A long and elegantly furnished hallway lies just behind the double-storey Portuguese-style façade of the house. It is lined with 28 bay windows and overlooks a well-maintained garden.

Baroque rosewood four-poster bed

3 Dining Hall
In the east wing, a rosewood dining table, meant to be an exact replica of the one at Buckingham Palace, fills the first floor dining hall of this sprawling mansion.

4 Chapel
The Braganza Pereira's private Baroque-style chapel in the east wing has a number of treasures including a gold-and-diamond-encrusted fingernail of St Francis Xavier *(see p27)* on its main altar.

5 Guest Bedroom
This room is dominated by a large rosewood four-poster bed. At its foot is a rosewood two-seater.

6 Stairway
A monumental double staircase forms the core of the house. The staircase connects the lower entrance level to the furnished top floors of the east wing, which comprise a series of interconnecting salons, dining halls, reception rooms, and the family's private chambers, ranged around a central courtyard.

7 Great Salon
The grandest room in the mansion is the Great Salon or ballroom. The walls as well as the floors are of Italian marble, and match the upholstry, while Belgian crystal chandeliers hang from the floral-patterned zinc ceiling. The highlight here is a pair of matching high-backed chairs, bearing the Braganza coat of arms, which was presented to the Braganza Pereira household by King Dom Luís of Portugal.

The splendid Great Salon

GOA'S PORTUGUESE ARCHITECTURE

Charming Sunaparanta, Goa Centre for the Arts

Goa's countryside is dotted with grand colonial mansions, built by wealthy land-owning Goan gentry. The homes of these local aristocrats were built in the traditional style of the region, with central courtyards, pyramidal *balcões* (porches) and unique oyster-shell window shutters. The furniture and interior decor, however, were largely European. Today, the beautiful Belgian chandeliers, Venetian cut-glass, gilded mirrors, antique Baroque-style rosewood furniture and Chinese porcelain, all displayed inside, provide a fascinating picture of the tastes and lifestyles of a vanished era.

TOP 10 INDO-PORTUGUESE HOUSES IN GOA

1 Figueiredo Mansion *(see p34)*, Loutolim

2 Salvador da Costa House, Loutolim

3 Roque Caetan Miranda House, Loutolim

4 Casa dos Mirandos, Loutolim

5 Sat Burnzam Ghor *(see p35)*, Margao

6 Loyola Furtado Mansion, Chinchinim

7 Braganza House *(see p34)*, Chandor

8 Palácio do Deão *(see p35)*, Quepem

9 Sunaparanta, Goa Centre for the Arts *(see p23)*, Altinho

10 Solar dos Colacos Ribandar

(8) Menezes Braganza Salon

The west wing opens into a salon. A collection of exquisite Chinese porcelain is displayed here, where a large vase takes pride of place.

(9) Library

With over 5,000 leather-bound books, mostly collected by renowned journalist and freedom fighter Luis de Menezes Braganza (1878–1938), the west wing library is considered one of Goa's finest and biggest private collections. There's also a set of four finely upholstered chairs called tête-à-têtes or love seats carrying their flamboyant owner's initials FXB (Francis Xavier Braganza).

(10) Family Portraits

A number of 17th- and 18th-century portraits of family

Portraits of family members

members can be seen around the house. A portrait of the grandfather of Luis de Menezes Braganza, Francis Xavier de Menezes Braganza, one of the few aristocrats to oppose Portuguese rule, hangs in the west wing ballroom.

TOP 10 ⭐ Palolem, Agonda and Around

Famous for its spectacular sunsets, Palolem is the ideal destination for a quiet holiday, away from central Goa's crowded beaches. North of Palolem is Agonda, which is peaceful than its neighbour, while Galgibaga has a beautiful stretch of virgin sand, shaded by casuarina trees. Also worth exploring is Rivona's Buddhist heritage and Usgalimal's prehistoric rock art. West of Palolem is Cotigao's wildlife sanctuary, known for its tranquil beauty.

1 Agonda Beach

This white sandy beach *(see p99)*, set between two cliffs, is a sought-after destination. It is famous as the nesting site for Olive Ridley turtles.

2 Palolem Island Reserve

Just off Palolem Beach, this island reserve has retained its biodiversity. Home to birds of prey, the island offers breath-taking ocean views. Dolphins or turtles can be spotted from a boat.

3 Cola Beach

To the north of Agonda is one of Goa's most secluded beaches, Cola *(see p48)*. Visitors can opt to stay in Rajasthani-style tent camps on the beach. There's also a freshwater lagoon here.

4 Butterfly Beach

A short ferry ride away from the Palolem coast this beach **(below)** takes its name from the exotic butterflies that can be spotted here *(see p100)*. It is known for its rich aquatic life and sunset views.

5 Netravali

This village is famous for its unique Bubble Lake. The Mainapi waterfall **(above)**, lies within a nearby wildlife sanctuary, which abounds in rich flora and fauna.

SILENT NOISE PARTIES

Palolem's lively party scene continues beyond Goa's 10pm amplified music ban thanks to the popular Silent Noise *(see p102)* headphone parties. The music is broadcast digitally to headsets during these parties. There's a choice of trance, house, electro and funk on different channels, synced with live AV screens, lights as well as lasers.

6 Galgibaga

A remote white sandy bay, Galgibaga or Turtle Beach (see p49) is one of best known nesting sites for Olive Ridley turtles. The northern end of the beach forms the turtles' habitat.

7 Rivona Buddhist Caves

These rock-cut caves, also known as Pandava Caves, were created in the 7th-century CE by Buddhist monks. The highlight here is the carved laterite *pitha*, the seat of the teacher.

10 Cabo da Rama

South of the fishing village of Betul is the Cabo da Rama (Cape Rama) promontory **(above)**. It is named after Rama, hero of the *Ramayana*, who is believed to have stayed here during his exile.

Palolem, Agonda and Around

Cuncolim
Betul
Rivona
Curdi
Cabo da Rama
Naquerim
Palolem
Canacona Chaudi
Jagvi

10
3
1
4
2
6
7
8
5
9

8 Usgalimal Rock Carvings

Hundred well-preserved petroglyphs, carved on laterite rock were found here in 1993. Believed to date back to the Stone Age, the carvings include birds and hunting scenes.

9 Cotigao Wildlife Sanctuary

Perfect for tree lovers, this vast reserve (see p100) of mixed deciduous woodland has plenty of birdlife **(left)**, but you are less likely to spot other wildlife here.

NEED TO KNOW

Agonda Beach & Cola Beach: **MAP D5**

Palolem Island Reserve & Butterfly Beach: **MAP D6**

Netravali: **MAP E5**

Galgibaga: **MAP D6**

Rivona Buddhist Caves: **MAP E5**

Cabo da Rama: **MAP D5;** Canacona; open 9am–5:30pm daily

Usgalimal Rock Carvings: **MAP E5**

Cotigao Wildlife Sanctuary: **MAP E6;** Canacona; 0832 296 5601; open 7am–5:30pm daily; adm

■ **Cabo da Rama** features the ruins of a Hindu fortress that fell to the Portuguese in 1763. The ramparts on the western side offer great views.

Top 10 Goa Themes

Splendid *reredos* with panels depicting scenes from the life of St Catherine at Sé Cathedral

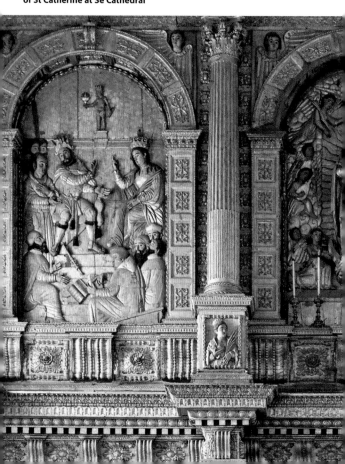

🔟 Moments in History

A scene from *Os Lusiadas*, depicting Vasco da Gama's arrival in Goa

① Mythological Goa

There are many legends about the creation of "Gomanta", "Govapuri", or present-day Goa. Despite the lack of historical evidence, Hindu mythology claims that Parashurama, an incarnation of god Vishnu, carved out this region after pushing out the sea with his arrows.

② Circa 300 BC: The Mauryas

Around this time, Goa was part of the Mauryan Empire under emperor Ashoka. He tried to convert the local people to Buddhism but after his death in 232 BC, much of these efforts fell flat as Goa was subsequently ruled by various Hindu dynasties for the next seven centuries. The Kadambas rose to power in AD 420, ushering in the first phase of the Golden Age of Goa.

③ 1352: The Sultanate

Years of tolerance and prosperity came to an end in 1352 as the Muslim Bahmanis took

A proselytizing priest during the Inquisition

over. This was followed by a period of religious and cultural persecution and all symbols of the Hindu Kadamba legacy were destroyed, except the temple in Tambdi Surla *(see p33)*.

④ 1498: Arrival of Vasco da Gama

Captained by Vasco da Gama, the Portuguese became the first Europeans to control trade routes to India. In 1543, after years of resistance, the sultan ceded large areas of Goa to them.

⑤ 1560: Golden Age to Goan Inquisition

By the end of the 16th century, the Portuguese Golden Age began. Their initial focus on trade was replaced by the arrival of the *Santo Officio* (Holy Office), better known as the Inquisition. One of the most brutal examples of cultural bigotry, it was conceived to target the "new Christians". Over the next 200 years, the Inquisition executed thousands of "heretics" of all faiths.

6 The Marathas

In 1664, the Portuguese temporarily lost a major part of their Goan territory to the Marathas, while the British continued to contest for the same. In 1739, in exchange for the Marathas withdrawal from Goa, the Portuguese were forced to sign a treaty and ceded large areas of their colony near Bombay.

7 1787: Pinto Revolt

Inspired by the propaganda used in the French Revolution, three priests from the Pinto clan conspired to overthrow the Portuguese. The plot was discovered, and the conspirators were tortured and executed, or sent away to Portugal.

8 1843: Old Goa to New Goa

New Goa (present-day Panaji) became the new official capital, leaving Old Goa deserted.

The first Republic Day after Liberation

9 Attempts at Liberation

Goa remained under Portuguese control even after India became independent in 1947. The Nehru government maintained that Goa, along with other Portuguese-occupied territories should be handed over to India. In 1961, after several requisitions to the Salazar regime failed, Indian troops marched in and were able to "liberate" Goa.

10 Present-day Goa

Since it was declared the 25th state of India in 1987, the tourism industry has flourished, making Goa a sought-after destination. In April 2019, Pramod Sawant was sworn-in as Chief Minister after the death of Manohar Parrikar while in office.

TOP 10 FAMOUS PERSONALITIES

Famous artist, Subodh Kerkar

1 Kesarbai Kerkar (1892–1977)
Awarded the Sangeet Natak Akademi award, she went on to become one of the most celebrated *khayal* (a kind of Indian classical vocal music) singers.

2 Deenanath Mangeshkar (1900–42)
This Hindustani classical vocalist was also a famous Marathi theatre actor.

3 Mario Miranda (1926–2011)
This famous cartoonist shot to fame after his work got published in *The Illustrated Weekly of India*.

4 Dilip Sardesai (1940–2007)
A former test cricketer, he is regarded as India's best batsman against spin.

5 Pundalik Naik (1952–)
The Sahitya Akademi award winner shot to fame with his novel *Acchev* (*The Upheaval*, 1977), the first Konkani novel to be translated into English.

6 Remo Fernandes (1953–)
A popular singer-composer, he was a big part of the Indi-pop music revolution of the 1990s.

7 Subodh Kerkar (1959–)
Aiming to make art more accessible for the masses, this eminent artist founded the Museum of Goa *(see p90)*.

8 Wendell Rodricks (1960–)
A fashion designer, environmental activist and a writer, he has restored his 450-year-old house and converted it to the Moda Goa Museum *(see p91)*.

9 Jayanti Naik (1962–)
Winner of the Sahitya Akademi award, this writer and translator is committed to the preservation of Konkani folklore.

10 Bruno Coutinho (1969–)
A former Indian football captain, he has received the Arjuna Award for outstanding achievement in the field.

🔟 Places of Worship

Gilded high altar at Sé Cathedral

in 1619. The central pediment and belfry were built later to accommodate the huge bell brought from Old Goa. The chapel in the south transept is dedicated to St Francis Xavier.

1 Sé Cathedral

The magnificent Sé Cathedral *(see p25)* has a Tuscan-style façade, flanked by a bell tower. The tower houses the Golden Bell, which rang out during the Inquisition's dreaded *auto da fé* trials, held in the front square. The *pièce de résistance* of the Corinthian interior is the altar, dedicated to St Catherine of Alexandria.

2 Church of Our Lady of the Immaculate Conception

This church *(see p20)* is Panaji's most distinctive landmark. The whitewashed Baroque façade of the present church and its twin towers were constructed

3 Church of St Cajetan

In the 17th century, Pope Urban III sent Italian priests from the Theatine Order to Golconda. They were refused entry there so they settled in Old Goa. In 1651, they erected a church *(see p25)* dedicated to their founder, St Cajetan, modelled on St Peter's in Rome. The dome and Baroque interior are in the form of a Greek cross.

4 Church and Monastery of St Augustine

Once the largest church *(see p24)* in India, with a five-storeyed façade, St Augustine's now lies in ruins. The church was abandoned in 1835, and excavations in 1989 revealed eight chapels and four altars. It is believed that in the 17th century there were also grand staircases, and a library that rivalled the one in Oxford. Today, all that remains is its bell tower.

5 Maruti Temple

MAP L3 ■ Nanu Tarkar Pednekar Rd, Altinho, Panaji ■ Open 6am–8pm

A striking edifice atop Altinho Hill, this temple looks beautiful at night when it is lit up. The presiding deity here is the monkey-god Hanuman who can be seen through a tiny hole in the basement wall.

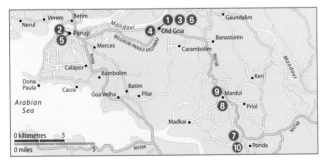

Baroque interior with floral frescoes at the Church of St Francis of Assisi

6 Church of St Francis of Assisi

A rare example of the Portuguese Manueline style, this church *(see p24)* has a beautifully carved doorway. A pair of navigator's globes and a Greek cross (the emblem of all Portuguese ships) embellish the door. The painted panels in the chancel depict scenes from the saint's life. The church is no longer used for worship.

7 Naguesh Temple

Dedicated to Lord Shiva, this temple *(see p30)* has an ancient water tank, built in a way that the reflection of the idol of Nagesh can be seen when standing at certain angles around the tank. The temple does not allow entry to foreigners.

8 Lakshmi Narasimha Temple

MAP D3 ■ Pharmacy College Rd, National Highway 4A, Ponda ■ Open 6:30am–12:45pm & 4:30–8:30pm daily

Surrounded by a forest, this is one of Goa's most attractive temples, with a sacred tank and an elaborate gateway. The majestic idol of Narasimha, Vishnu's man-lion incarnation, was brought here in the 1560s from South Goa's Salcete *taluka* (sub-district).

9 Manguesh Temple

A vividly painted elephant on wheels stands at the entrance to this 18th-century temple *(see p84)*, dedicated to Shiva. Inside, Belgian chandeliers hang from the ceiling, while the courtyard has a sacred *tulsi* (basil) plant growing in a green urn. There's also a seven-storeyed lamp tower here.

10 Shantadurga Temple

Goa's most popular shrine *(see p81)* was built by Shahuji, the grandson of Maratha chief Shivaji. This russet- and cream-coloured temple has an unusual pagoda-style roof, dominated by a five-storeyed octagonal lamp tower, unique to Goa. Embossed silver screens shield the main sanctuary, which houses the deity of Shantadurga (a form of Shiva's consort Parvati).

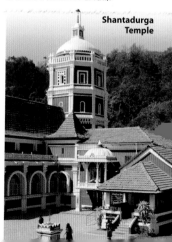

Shantadurga Temple

Beaches of North Goa

Shiva's face carved on rock, Vagator

1 Vagator

Beautiful Vagator's crescent-shaped bay is known for its small coves. The main beach (see p14) is split into Big and Little Vagator by a seaside headland. To the south is Ozran or Little Vagator, accessible by a steep path, which attracts partygoers in the evening. Its defining feature is the rock carving of Lord Shiva's face.

2 Candolim

Bustling Candolim (see p12) is usually the first stop for many before exploring the string of beaches along the north coast. Visitors can choose to unwind under parasols with a picnic basket or sample delicious food at the beach shacks. Water-skiing and parasailing are just some of the activities on offer here.

3 Calangute

Every year thousands of sunseekers from all over throng the sands of Goa's most famous beach, Calangute (see p16). Packed with restaurant shacks, nightclubs, shopping and accommodation options, there is a little bit of something for everyone here. It is also known for watersports.

Bridge leading to the shacks, Mandrem

4 Mandrem

A quiet fishing village with a beautiful location and a glorious beach (see p18), Mandrem's relaxed ambience is ideal for solitude-seekers. Small wooden bridges help visitors to cross a narrow creek that runs parallel to the coastline, and connects to the beach shacks, which line the shore.

5 Morjim
MAP H3

Secluded Morjim is a nesting site for Olive Ridley turtles. Sadly, sightings of the turtles even in the nesting season – between November and February – have become increasingly rare. The spot at the beach's southern end is great for birdwatching.

10 Querim
Paliyem
Korgao
Arambol 9
Mandrem 4
Parcem
Ashvem 8
Chopdem
Agarvada
Oxel
Morjim 5
Siolim
MDR 6
MDR 6
Vagator 1
Mapusa
Assagao
Anjuna 6
Parra
Arpora
Gurim
Arabian Sea
Baga 7
Saligao
Calangute 3
Dongarpur
0 km   4
0 miles   4
2 Candolim
Verem

Palm trees cover the headland overlooking the wide expanse of sea at Anjuna

6 Anjuna

Backed by swaying palms and low, rocky hills, Anjuna *(see p15)* has been a favoured vacation spot since the 1960s. In the evening, many places host parties with international DJs spinning everything from techno and hip-hop to current trance favourites. The crowds swell on Wednesdays during the flea market, which is a good place for souvenir shopping.

7 Baga

An extension of Calangute, Baga *(see p16)* is among the busiest beaches in North Goa. It is enduringly popular with watersport enthusiasts who can indulge in a wide range of activities such as jet-skiing, banana boat rides and water-skiing here. Baga's shores are populated with trendy eateries and bars, while its night-life is legendary due to the well-known Club Tito's *(see p94)*.

8 Ashvem

Goa's current hot spot, Ashvem *(see p18)* has become the place to soak up the sun, sand and surf. Its serene waters, eclectic beach shack restaurants, chic beachfront clubs and boutiques have made it the choice of celebrities. It is also known as one of the best spots to swim, dine and dance.

9 Arambol

Lively Arambol *(see p18)* has a freshwater lagoon that is fed by hot springs and is perfect for swimming. It is popular with those seeking active outdoor recreation and holistic therapies such as yoga and reiki, and is also known for its vibrant nightlife.

10 Querim

Tucked away at the northernmost tip of Goa far from the buzz of other beaches, gorgeous Querim (or Keri) is the ultimate hideaway. With its empty stretches of soft sand and clear waters *(see p19)* it is the ideal place for sunbathing and swimming.

Lovely, unspoiled beach at Querim

🔟 Beaches of South Goa

Scenic view of charming Cola Beach

① Cola

Also known as "Khola" beach, this is perhaps one of Goa's most beautiful beaches (see p38) with coconut groves and Rajasthani-style tents. The freshwater lagoon here, makes a great swimming spot. Consult a lifeguard for the best places to swim at the beach.

② Majorda

MAP A5 ■ Greenland Horse Racing: 9822586502
North of Colva, Majorda has a wide beach dotted with luxury hotels. Relatively crowd-free, this beach can be reached by crossing makeshift wooden bridges. It is the only place in Goa where visitors can ride a horse on the beach.

③ Mobor

MAP D5 ■ Betty's Place Boat Trips: www.bettysgoa.com
With its backdrop of jungle-covered hills, Mobor's golden white sands feature a number of luxury resorts including the famous Leela Goa (see p114). Visitors can go on river cruises as well as dolphin-spotting and birdwatching trips here.

④ Palolem

Enclosed by a rocky outcrop at one end, and Canacona Island, at the other, this crescent-shaped beach (see p97) is the loveliest in South Goa. It offers tree houses for rent and campsites at Canacona. Among its attractions are the boat rides offered by fishermen, who take visitors out to sea for dolphin-watching trips and spectacular sunset views. From November to March, the beach attracts crowds.

for windsurfing, and also has a diving school where visitors can opt for courses or guided dives to shipwrecks and coral reefs.

7 Benaulim
MAP A6

The roads of the quiet fishing village of Benaulim are lined with small guesthouses and beach shacks. The beach has Goa's largest fleet of wooden outriggers. A range of exciting watersports is on offer here.

8 Varca
MAP A6

The pristine white sands of Varca are perfect for lazing under the sun. Those keen to go out to sea can hop on to the boats of the local fishermen or simply go for a cruise along the River Sal to spot dolphins.

Turtle hatchlings at Galgibaga Beach

5 Betalbatim
MAP A5

Dotted with palm groves, serene Betalbatim is also called Sunset Beach. It is a good place to spend the day lounging on the beach and watching the sun set. Dolphins are easy to spot here.

6 Bogmalo

Surrounded by steep, wooded cliffs, little Bogmalo *(see p97)* is a hidden gem. An ideal family beach, its calm waters are generally safe for swimming. It is a popular venue

Idyllic palm-fringed Palolem Beach

9 Galgibaga

Fringed by towering casuarina trees, tranquil Galgibaga *(see p39)*, is a favoured breeding ground for the endangered Olive Ridley turtles. In November, the turtles lay their eggs, often on the same spot where they had hatched. The hatchling numbers though have decreased over the years.

10 Agonda

Picturesque Agonda *(see p99)* is great for lazing under the sun. Visitors can choose to enjoy a swim or engage in watersports, particularly canoeing, which is quite popular here. The turtle centre here helps conserve the Olive Ridley turtle eggs.

🔟 Outdoor Activities

1 Surfing

Surf Wala: www.surfwala. com ■ **Banana Surf School: www. goasurf.com**

Goa's beaches are mostly popular for surfing, although the sea here is also ideal for other watersports. There are a number of surfing schools, such as Vaayu Waterman's Village *(see p18)*, Banana Surf School and Surf Wala, which offer instruction for both beginners and experienced surfers.

Windsurfing, a popular beach activity

2 Scuba Diving and Snorkelling

Goa Diving: www.goadiving.com ■ **Dive Goa: 0932 503 0110** ■ **Goa Aquatics: www.goaaquatics.com**

While Goa's reefs may not be the best, there are still some great sites for diving and snorkelling such as Shelter Cove, Bounty Bay and Suzy's Wreck. Some of the main operators offer PADI (Professional Association of Diving Instructors) certification.

3 Rafting

Goa Rafting: 8805 727 230; www.goarafting.com

White-water rafting on the Mhadei River is a popular activity from June to September. Goa Rafting organizes trips in season at 9:30am and 2:30pm on Grade 2 and 3 (fairly easy) rapids.

4 Kayaking

Goa Kayaking: www.goa kayaking.com

Goa Kayaking offers kayaking excursions along the coast, rivers and backwaters of Goa throughout the year. Palolem's bay or Goa's several estuaries are considered best for kayaking.

5 Nature Walks

Goa Birding: 0855 408 0320 ■ **Goa Nature Trails: 0703 097 3005**

Goa offers plenty of nature excursions, birdwatching tours and camping expeditions from October to April. Some of the top birdwatching spots include Cotigao Wildlife Sanctuary *(see p39)*, Salim Ali Bird Sanctuary *(see p84)* and Bhagwan Mahavir Wildlife Sanctuary *(see p32)*.

6 Kitesurfing

Kitesurfing Goa: Montego Bay Resort, Morjim Beach; 0750 713 0099 www.kitesurfinggoa.com

An offshoot of windsurfing, kitesurfing is a dynamic form of wave-riding. Boards are short and the rider holds handles attached to cables and a kite. From January to April, Morjim Beach *(see p46)* is a major hub for this sport.

7 Stand Up Paddle Boarding (SUP)

Atlantis Watersports: www.atlantis watersports.com

This sport has gained plenty of popularity over the years, with boards tuition and guided paddles offered by schools. The ideal months for SUP is from October to May.

Hikers on a scenic trail in Netravali

Parasailing at Candolim Beach

(8) Parasailing
Explore Watersports® Goa: 0830 743 0073

Anjuna, Baga, Calangute, Vagator and Candolim beaches are great for parasailing. Participants sit in a sling seat attached to a specially designed parachute, which is hoisted skyward by a boat for fantastic views and an exhilarating ride. October to May is the best time for parasailing.

(9) ATV Rides
ATV Adventures Goa: 0982 306 8599

All-terrain vehicles are an exciting way to explore the muddy trails and off-the-beaten path sights. Wear sports shoes or closed-toe shoes.

(10) Hiking
Goa Jungle Adventure: www. goajungle.com

Several thrilling hiking options are available for adventurers to explore Goa's captivating landscapes. Some of the best trails are at Chorla Ghat *(see p84)*, Netravali *(see p38)* and Dudhsagar Falls *(see p32)*. Hiking is not advisable during the monsoons.

TOP 10 SPECIAL INTEREST ACTIVITIES

Go-Karting on a track in Goa

1 Go-Karting
The tracks in Nuvem village and Arpora are the best. Check www.gokarting goa.com for more information.

2 Soccer
Some of the Indian Super League matches (from November to March), are played at Fatorda Stadium. Goa's main professional football team is FC Goa.

3 Skateboarding
Panaji's Youth Hostel, ALIS Bowl in Morjim and Cirrus in Anjuna are popular skateboarding spots.

4 Horseback Riding
Majorda Beach is the only place where visitors can enjoy horseback riding.

5 Fishing
There are a number of boats that will take visitors out fishing for the day. Check www.johnboattours.com for fishing trips.

6 Eco Tours
For overnight camping tours at a wildlife sanctuary, check www.canopygoa.com and www.goaecotourism.com.

7 Diving
Bogmalo's diving schools offer PADI-approved open water courses and guided dives to shipwreck sites. Dive season runs from late October to April.

8 Boat Trips
Cruises of every sort are popular on the Mandovi, but the finest are the 1- or 2-hour sunset cruises.

9 Dolphin Spotting
Palolem, Morjim or Sinquerim are the best beaches to catch a glimpse of the Indo-Pacific humpback dolphin.

10 Bicycle Tours
Avid cyclists can opt for an interesting bicycle tour to explore Old Goa, Chorão and Divar Islands.

🔟 Children's Attractions

chutes or tubes. Rides such as the "Curly Wurly" water slide and the "Tad Pool" have been designed for small children.

3 Dudhsagar Falls

The country's second highest waterfall, Dudhsagar (see p32) on the Goa-Karnataka border, attracts plenty of visitors all year round. Only accessible on foot or by jeep, this is a popular trekking destination. Kids can go on a jungle safari, enjoy birdwatching or opt for a dip in the waters here.

1 Dolphin Spotting

Terra Conscious: www.terraconscious.com ▪ John Boat Tours: www.johnboattours.com

Some of the best beaches for dolphin spotting are Palolem, Sinquerim, Baga and Morjim. A number of operators such Terra Conscious and John's Boat Tours organize dolphin safaris.

2 Splashdown Water Park

MAP H4 ▪ Calangute–Anjuna Main Rd, Anjuna ▪ Open 10:30am–6pm ▪ Adm ▪ www.splashdowngoa.com

This water park boasts a number of high-velocity rides (multi-passenger as well as solo) down slides and

4 Goa Science Centre & Planetarium

MAP J6 ▪ Marine Highway, Miramar, Panaji ▪ Open 10am–6pm daily ▪ Adm ▪ www.goasciencecentre.org.in

The fantastic Goa Science Centre & Planetarium is the perfect place to experience a fun day. The science centre has two interactive galleries to explain the basic concepts of physics to kids. In addition, there is a 3D theatre and a dome-shaped planetarium. The outdoor park also has life-size models of dinosaurs.

Splashdown Water Park in Anjuna

5 Naval Aviation Museum

Goa's Naval Aviation Museum *(see p100)* boasts 15 types of aircrafts and exhibits such as scaled models of aircraft carriers, *INS Viraat* and *INS Vikrant*. The two-storeyed indoor gallery features rare photographs and information about key battles in which the Indian Naval and Air force participated. The evolution of the uniforms worn by Navy personnel are also well documented. The outdoor exhibits include several decommissioned aircrafts, which are on display in the museum's huge park.

Statues of craftsmen at work, Ancestral Goa

6 River Cruises

Goa Tourism Development Corporation (GTDC): 0832 243 8866; tickets at jetty or visit www.bookings. goa-tourism.com

A leisurely sunset river cruise *(see p20)* on the Mandovi is a wonderful way to take in Goa's sights. The cruise, the duration of which varies from an hour to two, usually begins from the jetty at the foot of the Mandovi bridge, every day between 6pm and 7pm. The entertainment on board is provided by Goan dancers and musicians. These cruises are also organized by several private operators in and around Goa.

7 Salim Ali Bird Sanctuary

This sanctuary *(see p84)* was named after Dr Salim Moizzudin Abdul Ali, one of the country's foremost ornithologists. In addition to colourful kingfishers and egrets, visitors may also spot the bulbous-headed mudskipper leaping above the water. The mangrove swamps can be explored by taking a boat ride in a dug-out canoe. It is best to visit early in the morning or just before sunset.

Kingfisher at Salim Ali Bird Sanctuary

8 Ancestral Goa

This unique model village *(see p35)* showcases Goan life and culture as it was a hundred years ago through miniature Portuguese colonial homes and life-size statues of tradesmen and craftsmen. Other attractions include the footprint of Big Foot on a rock and the longest laterite sculpture of Mirabai, a poet and devotee of Lord Krishna.

9 Butterfly Conservatory of Goa

Kids will enjoy being introduced to the colourful world of butterflies at the Butterfly Conservatory of Goa *(see p83)*. Founded by the Heblekar family, this tranquil conservatory with beautiful verdant surroundings is home to over 100 different butterfly species.

10 Spice Plantations

Central Goa's spice plantations *(see p30)* offer a delightful opportunity for a family day-out. Most of the spice farms in and around Ponda have guided tours in English, which is a wonderful way to learn about organically grown spices, herbs, fruits and crops. This is usually followed by a traditional Goan lunch buffet. July to March are the best months to visit the plantations.

⊤⚡️10 Nightlife

Dancefloor packed with revellers at Club Cubana, Arpora

1 Club Cubana
Perched on a hilltop, this multi-level open-air nightclub (see p94) is known as "the nightclub in the sky". There are several bar areas and the VIP section overlooks an impressive waterfall cascading into an underlit open-air pool. The music includes everything from house and techno to hip hop. Only couples are admitted; and there's even a ladies-only dance floor.

2 Hill Top
Set in a neon coconut grove, Hill Top (see p94) transforms into a prime destination for Goa's trance scene on some evenings. Apart from its wild New Year and Christmas rave parties, which span over three or four days, it is famous for its weekly Sunday sessions when international DJs spin psychedelic-trance beats until 10pm and on Fridays when the focus shifts to techno and house.

3 Club Tito's
Baga's legendary nightlife is mainly attributed to the iconic Tito's (see p94). Every Saturday night, revellers descend on the dance floor to enjoy pulsating retro and Bollywood hits. Guest DJs feature throughout the season. Next door is Mambo's, which gets packed with a lively crowd most nights. Hip-hop, and techno dominate after 11pm here.

4 Sinq Night Club
Created as a one stop destination for partygoers, Sinq (see p94) features four entertainment zones – a chic nightclub, a bistro with an Irish pub ambience, a poolside deck and private cabanas – that create the ultimate party venue. There's an open-air poolside lounge with a discotheque as well. Resident DJs spin mainstream dance tracks several nights a week.

5 SOMA Project
Fans of electronic music will not want to miss visiting this trendy beach club (see p94) with a lively

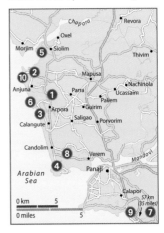

restaurant and a great cocktail bar on Ashvem Beach *(see p18)*. The resident DJs here keep the crowds on their feet by spinning their sets late into the night.

6 Shiva Valley

Known as the temple of trance, this large shack *(see p94)*, next to Curlies, attracts a huge crowd. Every Tuesday it remains packed mostly due to its psychedelic trance parties, which kick off from 5pm and continue well beyond midnight. Besides Tuesdays, Full Moon Night parties are also a big hit here. It has hosted big-name DJs, such as Earthling, Avalon, Tristan, Nigel, Ajja, Raja Ram.

7 Silent Noise

On a rock promontory at the southern end of Palolem Beach, Silent Noise *(see p102)* stages weekly headphone parties on Saturday nights. Put on a wireless headset and take your pick of either trance, house, hip hop, electro and funk played by three different DJs.

8 LPK Waterfront

MAP J6 ■ Nerul Rd, Opposite Bank of India, Nerul ■ 0932 673 3295 ■ Open 9:30pm–3:30am daily

Set against the backdrop of a 400-year-old church on the banks of the Nerul, LPK or Love Passion Karma is a fashionable Goan nightspot. Constructed mainly out of mud and stone, sculpted terracotta statues can be seen all around. Groove to the latest Bollywood hits here. The deck provides a great chill-out area.

9 Leopard Valley

One of the biggest open-air venues in India, Leopard Valley *(see p102)* is a high-octane nightclub featuring a 7-m (22-ft) high DJ stage. Groove to the best of EDM and Goa trance amid 3D laser light shows, pyrotechnics and firepits. The main parties are held here on Friday nights. Guest DJs include Eve Carey of Ministry of Sound fame, MV Cliff and Dan Booth.

Sea view from Chronicle

10 Chronicle

On the shores of Little Vagator and against the backdrop of the rocky Vagator cliffs, Chronicle *(see p94)* has a cocktail bar, Italian restaurant and an open-air dance floor, all impressively spread across five levels. The ground level, a multifunctional space, becomes a weekly outdoor dance floor. Music from deep house and tech to progressive pull in the crowds here.

Striking exterior of LPK Waterfront

📖 Goan Cuisine

① Xacuti

A staple found on the menu of most Goan restaurants is *xacuti*. The complex flavour that defines this chicken curry comes from the use of an elaborate number of spices and ingredients including poppy seeds, dessicated coconut and red chillies.

Fish prepared in *recheado* masala

② Recheado

Essentially a spice paste, the *recheado* is used to season seafood, usually mackerel, often prawns and pomfret. The whole fish is slit down the middle and cleaned, stuffed with flavoursome *recheado* and then fried in hot oil to be served as an appetizer. Some vegetables are also cooked using the same masala.

③ Cafreal

The chicken is usually marinated overnight with spices, such as ginger, garlic, onion, mace, cinnamon, green chillies and fresh coriander, the latter brings about its signature green colour. Fried or grilled the following day, this dish is accompanied by potatoes, lemon wedges and salad.

④ Sorpotel

An essential in any Goan celebration, the preparation for this stew begins days in advance as it is believed that the flavour of the curry gets better as it ages. Recipes differ from one kitchen to the other, but the traditional version is made from boneless pork and pork offal – liver, tongue, heart – though modern variations use other meat as well.

⑤ Bebinca

There are various stories regarding the origin of this dessert but Goans love their *bebinca* and it is widely accepted as the "queen" of Goan desserts. This traditional cake is prepared in layers (the numbers range from seven to 16) using simple ingredients such as plain flour, coconut milk, sugar, egg yolk and *ghee* (clarified butter).

⑥ Vindaloo

This curry came to India with the Portuguese and the name itself is a distortion of their popular dish *carne de vinha d'alhos*. The use of dry roasted spices such as mustard, fennel and coriander seeds plus red chillies (courtesy the Portuguese) and peppercorns gives the *vindaloo* its characteristic heat. The spice is balanced by the use of vinegar, tamarind paste and jaggery.

Portuguese-influenced pork *vindaloo* curry

Fiery prawn balchao

7 Balchao

The origins of *balchao* lie in Macau, which was once a Portuguese colony. A blend of chillies, ground spices and tomatoes is pickled with either coconut or *feni* vinegar, which lends the mixture its signature acidic taste. The paste is then used to make a curry with pork, fish or prawns.

8 Sanna

This steamed, spongy rice cake is a Goan staple that has two variants. The sweet *sanna* is made from jaggery and the plain savoury one is eaten as an accompaniment to curries or on its own.

Delicious caldeirada fish stew

9 Caldeirada

A cousin to the Greek *kakavia* and French *bouillabaisse*, this humble fishermen's stew uses a combination of lean and oily fish plus potatoes as a base, to give the dish a thick consistency. Shellfish and other seafood may be added along with vegetables.

10 Ambotik

True to its Konkani name (*ambot* means tangy and *tik* means spicy), this hot, sour and sweet fish curry is identified by its flaming orange colour due to the use of turmeric and Kashmiri chillies.

TOP 10 TRADITIONAL RESTAURANTS

1 Martin's Corner
MAP A5 ▪ 0832 288 0061 ▪ ₹₹₹
Sample Goan, Continental, Chinese and Indian fare at this multi-cuisine joint.

2 Anand Bar and Restaurant
MAP H4 ▪ 0989 055 8363 ▪ ₹₹
This place is popular with locals and tourists. Try the authentic fish *thali*.

3 Britto's
MAP H5 ▪ 0738 762 7948 ▪ ₹₹₹
This legendary shack has a great location by the beach.

4 Chef Fernando's Nostalgia
MAP B4 ▪ 0832 277 7098 ▪ ₹₹
Enjoy traditional Portuguese and Goan dishes plus great cocktails at this joint.

5 Joe Bananas
MAP H4 ▪ 0832 227 3459 ▪ ₹₹
Part of the hippie trail of the 1970s, this is an excellent place for Indian *thalis*.

6 O'Coqueiro
MAP K5 ▪ 0832 241 7806 ▪ ₹₹
Tuck into authentic *cafreal*, *xacuti*, *balchao* and *sorpotel* at this restaurant.

7 Anandashram
MAP L2 ▪ 0982 319 5245 ▪ ₹₹
A fish lover's delight, with fried fish, fish curry and fish *thali* on the menu.

8 Gunpowder
MAP J4 ▪ 0832 226 8083 ▪ ₹₹
An essential stop for those in the mood for coastal Indian cuisine.

9 Bhatti Village Family Restaurant and Bar
MAP J6 ▪ 0982 218 4103 ▪ ₹₹
This hidden gem is the perfect spot to try a home cooked Goan meal (see p91).

10 Viva Panjim
MAP L2 ▪ 0832 242 2405 ▪ ₹₹
Set in a converted 150-year-old house, Viva Panjim is a must visit for Goan food.

Charming Viva Panjim

For a key to restaurant price ranges see p79

⭐10 Places to Eat

Laid-back setting of Sublime, overlooking Morjim Beach

① Sublime

Celebrity chef Chris Saleem Agha Bee is at the helm of this restaurant *(see p95)*, in the heart of Morjim, which serves up flavours from around the world. Sample the fish carpaccio or ginger batter calamari. For mains, the Asiatic beef medallions with wasabi mash, the mega-organic salad or mustard-encrusted fish are good options.

② Thalassa

From ambience to food, this legendary open-air taverna *(see p95)*, set atop a rocky cliff, against a backdrop of swaying palms and the vast ocean beyond, offers everything Greek. Diners swear by the Thalassa lobster platter. Apart from seafood, they also serve great desserts – try the *baklava* (sweet and syrupy layered filo-pastry) or the cheesecake. Book a table in advance to catch the sunset views.

Diners at the popular Thalassa

③ Bomra's

Chef Bawmra Jap's award-winning restaurant *(see p95)* is Goa's best-kept secret. Bomra's serves superb contemporary Burmese and Kachin cuisine. Try the aromatic-flavoured pickled tealeaf sald and the snapper with lemongrass and galangal. The mojitos and desserts on the menu are great as well.

④ The Black Sheep Bistro

A welcoming yellow façade gives way to elegant dark-wood interiors at this popular restaurant *(see p79)*. Expect food that highlights fresh, local produce and goes well with their farm-to-table philosophy, promoting sustainable farming. While the red *kismoor* fish fillet is a favourite, there are many vegetarian options as well.

⑤ Sakana

Perfect for lovers of Japanese cuisine, Sakana *(see p95)* is close to Anjuna Beach. Generous portions and a well-priced menu make it great value for money. Sushi, sashimi and salads are favourites. The menu features plenty of vegetarian options too, including Udon bowls and miso soup.

⑥ A Reverie

Chic interiors, with a grand terracotta-tiled canopy and molecular gastronomy make this place *(see p95)* extra special. The desserts are spectacular, a spin on classics such as cheesecake and banoffee pie.

7 Café Nu

Launched in collaboration with chef Chris from Sublime, this relaxed café *(see p95)* in a garden setting offers fusion fare. Sample fish in banana leaves, the mega-organic salad, lemon cucumber, fig salad and lemongrass martinis.

8 Baba Au Rhum

Nestled in the quiet back roads between Anjuna and Baga, close to Bamboo Forest, Baba au Rhum *(see p95)* has a casual and laid-back vibe. Enjoy comfort food at this café cum restaurant serving salads, burgers, thin-crust pizzas and more. The bakery and patisserie are also popular.

Alfresco dining at Baba Au Rhum

9 Ourem 88

British couple Jodie and Brett run this quaint garden restaurant *(see p103)*. The menu offers Euro gastro dishes created from fresh, local produce, such as beef Wellington, pork belly, calamari stuffed with chorizo and steaks are excellent. Try the chocolate fondant and cheesecake.

10 Infantaria

Once Calangute's most famous bakery, Infantaria *(see p95)* now serves an impressive range of cuisines. The quiches, crepes and croissants from the bakery still remain bestsellers. The breakfasts at this charming terrace eatery are top-notch as well.

TOP 10 BEACHFRONT RESTAURANTS

1 La Plage
MAP G3 ▪ 0982 212 1712 ▪ ₹₹
French-run eatery offering tuna with wasabi mash, pumpkin ravioli and a delicious chocolate *thali*.

2 Zeebop by the Sea
MAP H2 ▪ 0832 275 5333 ▪ ₹₹
This shack serves superb, fresh seafood. Do try the fish curry with rice and crab papadums.

3 Surya Beach Café
MAP D6 ▪ 0992 315 5396 ▪ ₹
Sample all kinds of seafood – oysters, mussels, crab, lobsters, clams – at this little-known beachside shack.

4 Agonda White Sand
MAP D5 ▪ 0832 242 2405 ▪ ₹₹
The menu offers a variety of seafood, as well as Indian and European fare.

5 The Fisherman's Wharf
MAP D5 ▪ 0901 101 8866 ▪ ₹₹
Enjoy traditional Goan dishes such as prawn *balchao*, fish *reachado*, butter garlic prawns and crab curry at this legendary restaurant.

6 Dropadi Bar & Restaurant
MAP D6 ▪ 0832 264 4555 ▪ ₹₹
A mix of cuisines, with an emphasis on tandoori dishes are on offer here.

7 Olive Bar & Kitchen
MAP H4 ▪ 0788 803 7772 ▪ ₹₹₹
Tuck into the famous thin-crust pizzas, vegetarian mezze platters or the excellent seafood at this stylish multi-city restaurant chain.

8 Elevar
MAP G3 ▪ 0913 035 2188 ▪ ₹₹
Just as its name suggests, Elevar (or sublime in Portuguese) offers impressive contemporary and seasonal fusion fare.

9 Pousada by the Beach
MAP H5 ▪ 0992 227 9265 ▪ ₹₹₹
Experience delectable Portuguese, Goan and Konkan cuisine at this laid-back beach shack.

10 Prana Café
MAP H2 ▪ 0985 005 0403 ▪ ₹₹
Nutritious fare made from locally-sourced, fresh ingredients.

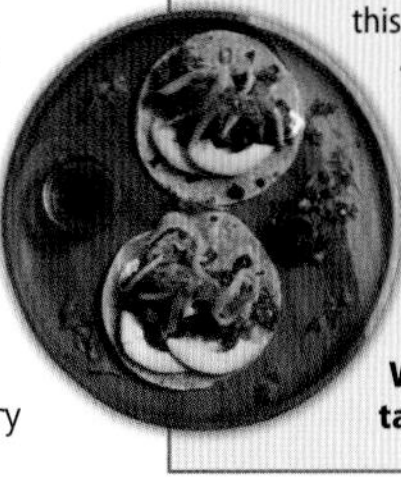

Wholesome fish tacos at Prana Café

For a key to restaurant price ranges see p79

🔟 Shops and Markets

The Arpora Saturday Night Bazaar

① Arpora Saturday Night Bazaar

Also known as Ingo's after the German expat who founded it, this popular night market *(see p93)*, held on a plot inland between Baga and Anjuna, bustles with energy. Spread over multiple levels, it is filled with colourful kiosks offering an array of items, such as apparel, spices, jewellery, handicrafts and a few real treasures for those prepared to hunt. In among the stalls, there are quirky bars, eateries serving tasty food and a stage featuring live music.

② Velha Goa Galeria

Next door to the Panjim Inn *(see p116)*, this store *(see p78)* specializes in exquisite traditional hand-painted *azulejos*, Portuguese tiles. The tiles are hand-painted by local artisans at the workshop in Aquem. Ceramic bowls, wall hangings, mirror frames and vases are also on sale here.

③ Anjuna Flea Market

The famous weekly flea market *(see p15)*, held every Wednesday, takes place at the southern end of the beach. It has a range of stalls selling everything from silver jewellery and souvenirs to Rajasthani mirrorwork and Kerela woodcarvings. Trendy beachwear round off the selection, while added attractions include fortune-telling Nandi bulls. Prices are high, so be sure to haggle to pick up things at a reasonable rate.

④ Solar Souto Maior

Housed in a 16th-century *palacio* believed to be the only surviving mansion from Goa's "Golden Age", the Solar Souto Maior *(see p78)* boasts an art gallery and a museum shop, which sells antiques and collectibles. It also has a delightful garden café.

⑤ Le Souk by Amarya

Inspired by the open-air bazaars of Morocco and the Middle East, this luxury market *(see p93)* has both local and international designer boutiques, housed in lavish tents. Visitors can enjoy a cup of coffee along with delicious crêpes at the café and Nespresso bar here.

⑥ Paper Boat Collective

One of Goa's most well-known boutiques, Paper Boat Collective *(see p93)* is housed in a beautiful Indo-Portuguese villa. It offers curated handcrafted products, ranging from ceramics and furniture to apparel.

Paper Boat Collective in Sangolda

Trendy lifestyle store, People Tree

7 People Tree

This iconic Delhi design store's *(see p93)* Goan outlet is housed in a century-old Goan villa in Assagao. It specializes in designing and producing handcrafted and artisanal products. The store is famous for its eclectic range of block prints, accessories, stationery and apparel.

8 Artjuna

Set in an old Portuguese villa, surrounded by a pretty garden, this lifestyle boutique *(see p93)* boasts a great collection of handmade leather bags, jewellery, accessories, clothes and home decor. There's also a charming outdoor Mediterranean café with a kids' play area and a yoga *shala*.

9 Mapusa Market

Though the market *(see p15)* is open all days, Fridays are special as local vendors and traders sell a range of spices, Goan pottery and the spicy *chouriço* sausages in the covered colonnades in front of the rows of shops. In the lanes leading off from the main market are stalls selling handicrafts and souvenirs from all over the country.

10 The Attic

Collectors of antiques would not want to miss visiting The Attic *(see p93)*. It is known for its great collection of furniture and Goan antiques, which include intricate glassware as well as wooden chairs and candlesticks.

TOP 10 THINGS TO BUY

1 Azulejos
These beautiful Portuguese hand-painted tiles make a fine souvenir.

2 Bebinca
This traditional multi-layered dessert *(see p58)* of Portuguese origin is a treat worth buying to carry back.

3 Feni and Port Wine
The famous local speciality *feni* comes in cashew and coconut flavours. Another must-buy is the Goan port wine.

4 Spices
An essential ingredient in Goa's fiery cuisine, spices such as cardamom, clove and cinnamon are widely available.

5 Cashew nuts
Introduced by the Portuguese in Goa in around 1560, cashews are ubiquitous.

6 Pottery and Terracotta
Shop for statues of terracotta soldiers and cockerels that can be seen on the gates of traditional Goan houses, from Bicholim or Mapusa Market.

7 Jute Macramé
Buy jute lamp shades, flower pots and hangers at the boutiques in Goa.

8 Kunbi Saree
A cotton chequered saree *(see p90)* with a sturdy weave to withstand farming, it was worn by tribal women before the arrival of the Portuguese in Goa.

9 Chitari Woodcraft
The painted and lacquered furniture from the Chitari craftsmen in Cuncolim is worth looking out for.

10 Art and Antiques
Cartoonist Mario Miranda's sketches are available at galleries in Panaji and North Goa. Indo-Portuguese antiques and impressive hand-painted ceramics can be found in stores scattered across the state.

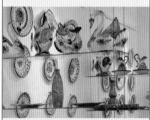

Ceramics at Velha Goa Galeria

Following pages Beautiful palm-fringed sandy Cola Beach

TOP 10 Goa for Free

The imposing Church of St Cajetan in Old Goa

1 Old Goa

Located 10 km (7 miles) east of Panaji, Old Goa (see pp24–7) was built in the 15th century by the Adil Shahi dynasty of Bijapur. The port city was captured by the Portuguese in the early 16th century, but abandoned due to a plague in the 18th century. Today, the remains of the city are a UNESCO World Heritage Site.

Idyllic setting of Vagator Beach

2 Beaches

With endless stretches of sand Goa is a beach-lover's paradise. The happening beaches of North Goa (see pp46–7) buzz with life and offer Konkan cuisines, snacks, cocktails and mocktails. The beaches of South Goa (see pp48–9) are ideal for those in search of a bit of peace and quiet.

3 Fort Aguada

Overlooking the Arabian Sea, the well-preserved 17th-century Fort Aguada (see p12) was constructed to defend against attacks by the Marathas and Dutch. The fort got its name (aguada means water) from the freshwater spring within the fort that provided water to the ships that docked here.

4 Churches

Goa boasts some of the oldest churches in India and they showcase an amazing blend of Portuguese and Indian architecture. Among the more famous ones are the Basilica de Bom Jesus (see p24), Sé Cathedral (see p25), Church of St Francis of Assisi (see p24), Church of St Cajetan (see p25) and the Church of Our Lady of the Immaculate Conception (see p20).

5 Fontainhas

Cut off from Panaji's din, Fontainhas (see p20) is Goa's Latin Quarter. It offers a walk that is an experience in itself. The Portuguese influence is evident from the architecture. Look out for the narrow winding and tapered streets, flanked by old villas with tiled roofs and buildings painted in the traditional colours.

6 Goa Carnival

Celebrated since the 18th century, the boisterous Carnival (see p68) is Goa's most famous festival. It is believed that Goa comes under the rule of King Momo who encourages all to eat, drink and make merry.

7 Flea Markets

Arpora's Saturday Night Bazaar (see p93) is among the best places to shop for handicrafts, fashion apparel, rugs, accessories, designer jewellery, herbs and spices as well as a quick bite or a delicious meal. The weekly Anjuna Flea Market (see p15), which is open until sunset, is another great option too.

8 Dudhsagar Falls
This majestic four-tiered waterfall (see p32), among India's tallest, is located on the Mandovi River. The best way to reach the falls is by car via Colem. For those looking for more adventure, trekking is an option too.

9 Public Astronomical Observatory
Set up by the Association of Friends for Astronomy in 1990, the Public Astronomical Observatory (see p23) is an ideal place for amateur astronomers and stargazers. Owing to its seaside location and the lack of tall buildings, the view of the sky can be astounding. One can simply go for stargazing and beach astronomy, or attend the science film festival organized by the AFAO.

10 Mario Gallery
Discover how history shaped Goa through the years in signature Mario Miranda's style. His artworks are used on various articles such as crockery, T-shirts, postcards and illustrated books. These can be bought as souvenirs (see p16).

Souvenirs for sale at Mario Gallery

TOP 10 BUDGET TIPS

Motorbikes for hire

1 A convenient option for travelling around Goa is by gearless motorbikes, which can be rented easily (see p106).

2 Motorcycle rickshaws are a cheap mode of transport in Goa.

3 Skip conventional restaurants and try the beachfront restaurants (see p61) that Goa is famous for. They offer affordable and delicious food options that range from continental to local cuisine.

4 Various mobile apps offer online table reservation services plus discounts and cashbacks on restaurant bills. Dineout is a popular app that works for both Android and iOS. Set lunches and buffets as well as weekend brunches at popular restaurants can be very good value and cost less than the evening meals.

5 Many bars and pubs have "Ladies Nights" on weekdays where entry and drinks are free for women.

6 Most bars have happy hours during early evenings (usually 5–8pm) that offer "one plus one" on drinks as well as spirits.

7 Alcohol is cheaper in wine shops compared to in restaurants, bars or beach shacks.

8 Test your bargaining skills at local markets (see pp62–3) – you might get a good deal off the original quote.

9 Everything from room rates to food is cheaper during the off season months – April to October.

10 If you want to try your hand at gambling, visit the casinos on weekdays. The prices usually go up over the weekends from Friday to Sunday.

🔟 Festivals

1 Three Kings Feast
6 Jan or first Sun in Jan

Grand processions take place at the Three Kings Church *(see p97)* during the *Festa dos Reis* (Three Kings Feast). Young boys from local villages re-enact the Three Magi blessing baby Jesus and are accompanied by crowds to Remedios Hill.

Church lit during Three Kings Feast

2 Shantadurga
Jan

During this famous festival, a silver statue of Hindu goddess Shantadurga *(see p81)* is carried in procession between the villages of Fatorpa and Cuncolim. It is also known as the "Procession of the Umbrellas", as it is led by 12 umbrellas, which represent different communities.

3 Goa Carnival
Pre-Lent

Goa's grandest festival is celebrated before Lent. It begins in Panaji with the crowning of King Momo, the king of chaos and fun. The parade has elaborate floats and masked revellers in fancy dress. Three days and nights of nonstop revelry follow, which ends at Vasco da Gama.

4 Shigmotsav (Shigmo)
Feb/Mar

A Goan rendition of the popular Hindu festival of colours, Holi, Shigmo features traditional folk dances and street floats depicting mythological and religious scenes. Highlights include the *Ghodemundi* during which men perform a martial dance with wooden horses strapped to the lower half of their bodies.

5 Sao Joao
Jun

This feast celebrates the arrival of the monsoon and honours the baptism of St John the Baptist. To mark this event, young people jump into lakes and ponds, and boat races are organized in Siolim *(see p15)*.

6 Bonderam
Fourth Sat in Aug

The Bonderam festival takes its name from *bandeira*, which means flag in Portuguese. Held on Divar Island *(see p82)*, it commemorates the Portuguese system of using flags to indicate property boundaries between feuding villagers. Mock

The colourful, festive annual Goa Carnival parade

Flag bearers at the start of Bonderam

fights are re-enacted to knock down the flags. Parties begin and bands strike up a tune from 7pm.

7 Narkasur Parades
Oct; Eve of Diwali

To celebrate the victory of the Hindu god Krishna over the demon Narkasur effigies of the demon are burned. This is meant to symbolize the victory of good over evil and heralds the festival of lights, Diwali.

8 Feast of St Francis Xavier
3 or 4 Dec

The feast of Goa's patron saint is held on the anniversary of his death. Attended by pilgrims from all over the world, the feast is preceded by *novenas* (nine days of prayer).

9 Feast of Our Lady of the Immaculate Conception
Early Dec

This holy feast is celebrated at the famous Church of Our Lady of the Immaculate Conception *(see p20)* to commemorate Mother Mary's conception. Festivities go on for a few days and street stalls are set up around the church. In the evening, there are firework displays.

10 Christmas and New Year
25 Dec–1 Jan

During the festive season, the streets and most churches across the state are beautifully decorated with lights. The Christmas eve Midnight Mass is traditionally known as *Misa de Galo*, (Cock's Crow) as it continues until dawn. On New Year's Eve, numerous beach parties are held accompanied by great firework displays.

TOP 10 EVENTS IN GOA

1 International Kite Festival
Two-day festival, including night kite flying at Miramar Beach (Jan).

2 Sensorium
Exhibition of arts, cinema and music at Sunaparanta, Goa Centre for the Arts (Jan–Mar, see p23).

3 Monte Music Festival
A cultural event for lovers of classical music and dance organized by Cidade de Goa and Fundação Oriente (Feb).

4 Grape Escapade
Four-day wine festival in Panaji with culinary delights, grape stomping and wine tasting sessions (Apr).

5 International Film Festival of India
India's largest film festival celebrates cinema by hosting screenings of Indian and international films (Nov).

6 Goa International Jazz Live Festival
Celebration of contemporary jazz showing performances by India's finest bands as well as international acts (Dec).

7 Serendipity Arts Festival
Multi-disciplinary event held at the Old Secretariat *(see p22)* on the banks of the Mandovi River (Dec).

8 Goa Arts & Literary Festival (GALF)
Goa's literary and art festival features diverse writers, artists and musicians from all over the world (Dec).

9 Liberation Day
Military parades mark the liberation of Goa from Portuguese rule (17th Dec).

10 Zagor Festival
Siolim's main festival includes midnight processions bearing the effigy of the village deity Zagoryo, followed by a dance drama re-enacted by members of two old Siolim families (Dec).

International Kite Festival

🔟 Excursions from Goa

Stunning waterfall in Amboli

1 Amboli
Maharashtra, 90 km (56 miles) from Panaji ■ Bus or car

Blessed with numerous waterfalls, this hill station is fondly called the "Queen of Maharashtra". A perfectly peaceful retreat, Amboli is among the world's top eco hot-spots and is flush with unusual flora and fauna. Amboli Falls, Shirgaonkar Point, Madhavgad Fort and Hiranya Keshi Temple, are definitely worth a visit.

2 Chorla Ghat
Goa's hills (ghats) are just as beautiful as its beaches, with Chorla Ghat (see p84) being just one such example. Located on the Karnataka border in the Western Ghats, this area is ideal for jungle walks, treks and hikes.

3 Sawantvadi
Maharashtra, 62 km (39 miles) from Panaji ■ Train & bus

Located a short drive away from Panaji is the pretty little town of Sawantvadi. It has a palace named after the erstwhile rulers of the state, Khem Sawant. The current queen still lives in the palace with her family and promotes local arts such as woodwork painting. Work-shops held in the palace attract locals and tourists. Moti Talao and Raghunath market merit a visit.

4 Dandeli
Maharashtra, 100 km (62 miles) from Panaji ■ Train & bus

An ideal place for outdoor enthusiasts, Dandeli has abundant wildlife and the sanctuary is home to diverse flora and fauna. Safaris, white-water rafting, canoeing, kayaking, rapelling, mountain biking and trekking are some of the activities available here.

5 Hampi
Karnataka, 347 km (216 miles) from Panaji ■ Train & bus

A UNESCO World Heritage Site, Hampi is known for its architecture and history. Among the places

from Panaji, and Divar can be reached from Old Goa through short ferry rides. Go bird watching at the Salim Ali Bird Sanctuary (see p84); walk or cycle through the picture perfect countryside dotted with elegant Portuguese villas and visit a small church at Divar.

8 Fort Tiracol
MAP G1 ■ 42 km (26 miles) from Panaji ■ Ferry from Querim

Once an armed fortress of the Portuguese, Fort Tiracol is now a heritage hotel (see p121) located on a cliff, offering breathtaking views of the Arabian Sea and Tiracol River.

to visit are the many temples, palace ruins, royal pavilions and ancient markets, along the Tungabhadra River, dating back to the Vijayanagara Empire.

6 Nersa
Karnataka, 113 km (70 miles) from Panaji ■ Train & bus

An off-the-beaten track village rich in biodiversity, Nersa is a haven for ornithologists. It is home to over 250 birds and 950 bat species. It is perfect for trekking too.

7 Chorão & Divar Islands
These two islands (see p82) are ideal to get a feel of rural Goa. Chorão Island can be accessed from Ribandar, a short drive away

Gigantic Shiva statue in Gokarna

9 Gokarna
Maharashtra, 164 km (102 miles) from Panaji ■ Car or bus

With its quiet beaches, beautiful temples and good food, Gokarna is a quaint town with a unique culture. Visit the iconic Om beach or Kudle, Paradise, Half Moon and Gokarna beaches. It is the perfect place for jet skiing, dolphin spotting, and fishing or simply for a stroll along the coast.

10 Vengurla
Maharashtra, 65 km (70 miles) from Panaji ■ Train & bus

The charming town of Vengurla is known for its temples, rocks, white sand beaches, mango and cashew plantations and folk art known as Dashavtara. Watersports facilities are available and seafood is abundant.

Virupaksha Temple, Hampi

Goa
Area by Area

The enchanting Great Salon
of Braganza House

TOP 10 Panaji and Old Goa

The Mandovi River serves as a beautiful backdrop to the current and former capitals of Goa, Panaji and Old Goa respectively. Full of colonial charm, Panjim – officially known by its Maharashtrian name Panaji, which means "land that does not flood" – retains an old-fashioned character, which is evident in its grand colonial era buildings and backstreets of the atmospheric Latin Quarter, Fontainhas. Linked to modern Panaji by a centuries-old causeway is Old Goa, once known as "Golden Goa" for its incredible prosperity. Foremost among the attractions here are its iconic Baroque churches, which have been classified as UNESCO World Heritage Sites. Nearby is lively Miramar Beach and quiet Dona Paula, replete with legends and known for its breathtaking sea views.

Statue at the Bishops Palace

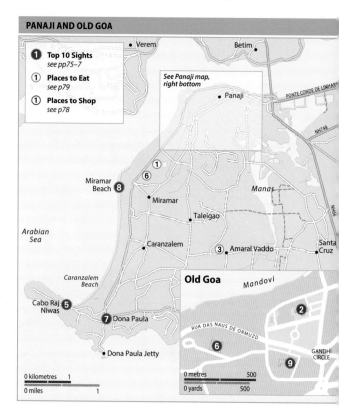

PANAJI AND OLD GOA

1 **Top 10 Sights**
see pp75–7

1 **Places to Eat**
see p79

1 **Places to Shop**
see p78

Verem

Betim

See Panaji map, right bottom

Panaji

PONTE CONDE DE LINHAR

NH4B

Miramar Beach ⑧

Manas

Miramar

Taleigao

NH66

Arabian Sea

Caranzalem

③ Amaral Vaddo

Santa Cruz

Caranzalem Beach

Old Goa

Mandovi

Cabo Raj Niwas ⑤

②

RUA DAS NAUS DE ORMUZD

⑦ Dona Paula

⑥

GANDHI CIRCLE

• Dona Paula Jetty

⑨

0 kilometres 1
0 miles 1

0 metres 500
0 yards 500

1 Church of Our Lady of the Immaculate Conception

Overlooking Panaji's main square is the iconic Church of Our Lady of the Immaculate Conception (see p20), built in 1541. The impressive double flight of stairs leading up to the church was added in 1871. The Baroque splendour of the main altar and the two transept altars is in sharp contrast to the otherwise simple interior.

Altar of a chapel at Sé Cathedral

2 Sé Cathedral

Ordered by the government in Portugal to build a church worthy of their mighty empire, Francis Coutinho (Viceroy, 1561–1564) envisaged a magnificent cathedral that would be the largest in Asia. The result is the Renaissance-style Sé Cathedral

(see p25). Its façade was flanked by two square bell towers, only one of which survives. In it hangs the Golden Bell, known for its melodic tones. The interior features a gilded high altar, dedicated to St Catherine of Alexandria, with panel paintings depicting scenes from her life.

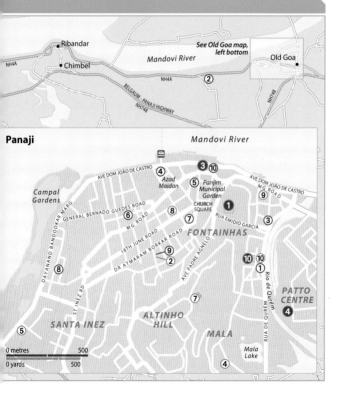

Ribandar
Chimbel
Mandovi River
See Old Goa map, left bottom
Old Goa
NH4A
NH4A
BELGAUM – PANAJI HIGHWAY
NH748
NH748
(2)

Panaji
Mandovi River

AVE DOM JOÃO DE CASTRO
(4) Azad Maidan
(3)(10)
(5) Panjim Municipal Garden
AVE DOM JOÃO DE CASTRO
M G ROAD
(9)
Campal Gardens
GENERAL BERNADO GUEDES ROAD
(6)
M G ROAD
(8)
CHURCH SQUARE (1)
RUA EMIDIO GARCIA
(3)
(7)
FONTAINHAS
DAYANAND BANDODKAR MARG
18TH JUNE ROAD
DR ATMARAM BORKAR ROAD
(9)(2)
AVE PADRE AGNELO
(10)(10)(1)
(8)
ST INEZ RD
(7)
RIO de Ourem
PATTO CENTRE
RUA DE QUEREM
(4)
(5)
SANTA INEZ
ALTINHO HILL
MALA
Mala Lake

0 metres 500
0 yards 500
(4)

A street in Fontainhas flanked by brightly coloured Indo-Portuguese houses

③ Fontainhas

The capital's oldest and most colourful district, Fontainhas *(see p20)* is known for preserving the ambience of colonial times. Street names such as Rua 31 de Janeira (31st January Road) signify Portugal's independence from Spain, while 18th June Road commemorates the end of Portuguese rule in Goa. Look out for colour-washed houses and *azulejo* street signs.

④ Goa State Museum

MAP M2 ■ EDC Complex, Patto ■ 0832 243 8006 ■ Open 10am–6pm Mon–Sat

Established in 1977, this museum preserves Goa's rich history. It houses a collection of pre-colonial artifacts, including statues, sati stones, carvings from ravaged Hindu temples, as well as some Christian icons. Look out for the furniture used by the Portuguese.

⑤ Cabo Raj Niwas

In 1760, this building *(see p22)* became the official residence of the viceroys – until 1918. Extensive renovations have transformed the original Islamic structure into the colonial building it is today, with a sloping tiled roof, wide wooden verandahs and cast-iron pillars. The Ashoka Chakra, the emblem of the Indian government, has replaced the Portuguese viceroys' coat of arms above the entrance.

⑥ Museum of Christian Art

MAP L6 ■ Convent of Santa Monica, Velha Goa ■ 0832 228 5299 ■ Open 9:30am–5pm Mon–Sat

Asia's first Museum of Christian Art was established in 1991 by the Indian National Trust for Art and Cultural Heritage (INTACH) and the Gulbenkian Foundation of Portugal. The impressive collection includes 17th- and 18th-century religious objects such as silver and ivory ornaments, ornate clerical robes, processional crosses and holy water sprinklers.

⑦ Dona Paula

MAP D6

About 7 km (4 miles) southwest of Panaji, Dona Paula is located near the

---

THE GOAN INQUISITION

At the request of Francis Xavier, a tribunal of Jesuits arrived in 1560. Their mission was to curb the libertine ways of the Portuguese settlers and convert "infidels". Those who refused were locked away in the dungeons of the "Palace of the Inquisition" (as Adil Shah's palace was known) to await the *auto da fé* (acts of faith) trials. The condemned were burnt alive in front of a congregation of dignitaries. Over the next 200 years, 16,000 trials were held and thousands were killed, and it was not until 1812 that the Inquisition was finally dissolved.

headland dividing the estuaries of the Zuari and Mandovi rivers. According to legend, it is named after a viceroy's daughter who, it is believed, jumped into the sea when she wasn't allowed to marry a local fisherman. The jetty offers views of Fort Aguada, across the bay, and is especially beautiful during sunset. Jet skis are available for rent, and visitors can also take a ferry ride to Vasco da Gama harbour.

8 Miramar Beach
MAP K6

Panaji's nearest beach, Miramar is about 3 km (2 miles) west. Named Porta de Gaspar Dias by the Portuguese, this beach is a busy spot especially during the evenings. Several food trucks and shacks offer streetside snacks here.

Popular sands of Miramar Beach

9 Basilica de Bom Jesus

Built by the Jesuits in 1594, this church (see pp24–7) is home to the world-famous mausoleum of Francis Xavier, Goa's patron saint.

10 Indian Customs & Central Excise Museum
MAP L1 ■ Avenida Dom João de Castro, Ozari, Panaji ■ 0982 366 5719 ■ Open 9:30am–5pm Tue–Sun

Housed in a striking blue heritage building, this museum offers an insight into the history of the customs and excise departments in India. The museum has four galleries, which showcase an array of seized goods and antiques. On display are items such as the gilded idol of Jambala that was smuggled into India from Nepal.

A DAY IN PANAJI AND OLD GOA

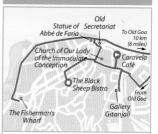

▶ MORNING

A good way to get a feel of Goa's Portuguese ambience is by spending some time in Panaji, which is ideally located on the banks of the Mandovi River. Begin your morning with a cup of coffee at the **Caravela Café** (see p79) before heading to the nearby **Gallery Gitanjali** (see p20), an arts and cultural centre that displays works by national and international artists. Next, stop at the distinctive **Church of Our Lady of the Immaculate Conception** (see p75), an important landmark. Allow yourself an hour here. Then enjoy a riverside stroll along the Mandovi, passing attractions such as the **Old Secretariat** (see p22) and the striking **Statue of Abbé de Faria** (see p20) along the way. Next stop for lunch at **The Fisherman's Wharf** (see p61). Sample local and European cuisine here.

AFTERNOON

After lunch, enjoy a drive along the Mandovi River to the Basilica de Bom Jesus and Sé Cathedral (see p75) in Old Goa (see pp24–7). The basilica is revered by Catholics from all over as it is home to the mortal remains of Goa's patron saint, Francis Xavier. It is advisable to dress conservatively when visiting. From Old Goa hop on board a bus to Panaji's Kadamba Bus Stand. Then take a short stroll along the bustling 18th June Road, which will lead you to **The Black Sheep Bistro** (see p79), popularly known as BSB. The globally inspired menu features dishes made with local ingredients.

See map on pp74–5 ←

Places to Shop

① Velha Goa Galeria
MAP M2 ■ Rua de Ourém, Panaji ■ Open 10:30am–7:30pm Mon–Sat

An iconic store *(see p62)* in Goa's Latin Quarter, which specializes in traditional hand-painted *azulejos*.

② Solar Souto Maior
MAP M6 ■ B-40, Maior Sao Pedro, Old Goa ■ Open 9:30am–6:30pm daily

This heritage house *(see p62)* is an art gallery and a museum-shop displaying chandeliers, wall hangings and more.

③ Sosa's
MAP M2 ■ E-245, Rua de Ourém, Panaji ■ 0832 222 8063 ■ Open 10:30am–7pm Mon–Sat

Shop for apparel by reputed designers such as Aki Narula, Rahul Mishra and Gaurav Gupta.

④ Aparant Goan Handicrafts Emporium
MAP L1 ■ Crafts Complex, Malacca Rd, Panaji ■ 0832 222 4478

This emporium promotes a variety of handicrafts such as woollen tapestries and carpets made by local artisans.

⑤ Mario Gallery
MAP L1 ■ Below Aroma Hotel, Duarte Pacheco Rd, Panaji ■ 0832 242 1776

Artworks of Goa's most celebrated artist, Mario Miranda, can be found here. The store offers various collectibles and his famous illustrations.

Prints for sale at Mario Gallery

⑥ Marcou Artifacts
MAP M2 ■ Casa Rocha, 31st January Rd, Panaji ■ 0832 222 0204 ■ www.marcouartifacts.com

This quirky store is known for its beautifully handcrafted souvenirs and ceramic decorative items made by local artisans.

⑦ Khadi Gramodyog Bhavan
MAP L2 ■ Municipality Building, Atmaram Borkar Rd, Panaji ■ 0832 223 2746 ■ Open 9am–7pm Mon–Fri

The Khadi and Village Industries Commission's emporium offers hand-made cottons, oils, soaps and spices.

⑧ Wendell Rodricks Design Space
MAP K2 ■ 158, near Luis Gomes Garden, Panaji ■ 0832 223 8177

The flagship store of designer Wendell Rodricks stocks an organic clothing line for men and women.

⑨ Sacha's Shop
MAP L2 ■ Swami Vivekananda Rd, Panaji ■ 0832 222 2035 ■ Open 10am–8pm Mon–Sat (from noon Sun)

Sacha Mendes's boutique has stylish Goan resort wear, statement jewellery, and bags. It also has designer labels.

⑩ Galeria Azujelos De Goa
MAP L1 ■ Next to Sales Tax Office, Panaji ■ 0982 297 6867 ■ Open 10am–7pm Mon–Sat

Set inside Orlando de Noronha's 250-year-old home, this unique shop is ideal for gifts and souvenirs.

Places to Eat

PRICE CATEGORIES
For a meal for two, including taxes and
service charge but not alcohol.
....
₹ under ₹700 ₹₹ ₹700–₹1500
₹₹₹ over ₹1500

1 Mum's Kitchen
MAP J6 ■ 854, Martins Building,
D B St, Panaji ■ 0982 217 5559 ■ ₹₹₹
Dishes here are recreated from old
family recipes collected from across
the state. The *kombdechem sukhem*
(spicy boneless chicken) is a speciality.

2 The Black Sheep Bistro
MAP L2 ■ Swami
Vivekanand Rd,
Panaji ■ 0832
222 2901 ■ ₹₹₹
In BSB's *(see
p60)* sophisticated
dining room, a savvy
take on globally inspired
cuisine is the order of the
day. Try their cocktails.

**The Black
Sheep Bistro**

3 Peep Kitchen
MAP K6 ■ Risara Luxury, Ground
Floor, Taliegao Market Rd, Panaji
■ 0880 617 0123 ■ Closed Mon ■ ₹₹
Through its food, this eatery focuses on
reviving old recipes and disappearing
culinary traditions. The prawn masala
fry and fish *recheado* are favourites.

4 Barrel & Bones
MAP L3 ■ 49, Fontainhas,
Panaji ■ 0777 408 276 ■ ₹₹
This intimate and rustic steakhouse
is known for its generous portions
of masterfully prepared steaks. Try
the famed Goan sausage pizza too.

5 Tao
MAP K6 ■ A-1, Dr Gama Pinto
Rd, Panaji ■ 0787 507 9242 ■ ₹₹₹
A classy restaurant, Tao has rustic
stonewalls, a pebbled bar and
bamboo slated lighting. The menu
offers Cambodian, Chinese, Balinese,
Singaporean and Korean specialities.

6 Oak Barrel
MAP J6 ■ Dayanand
Bandodkar Marg, Miramar ■ 0832
246 4330 ■ Closed Tue ■ ₹₹
Sample delicious Thai and Chinese
cuisine in a relaxed setting at
Oak Barrel. Enjoy hearty portions
of dim sums, Taipei chicken and
the sushi platter.

7 Café Bodega
MAP L2 ■ 63/C-8, Sunaparanta,
Goa Centre for the Arts, Panaji ■ 0832
242 1315 ■ Closed Sun ■ ₹₹
An alfresco café set in the
courtyard of an art gallery,
Café Bodega is the
perfect spot to
enjoy break-
fast. The
Vietnamese
coffee is not
to be missed.

8 Ritz Classic
MAP L2 ■ 10678,
1st floor, Wagle Vision
Building, 18th June Rd,
Panaji ■ 0832 242 6417 ■ ₹
The flavour-packed food and
competitive prices draw in a steady
stream of diners through the day.
Don't miss the fish *thali* (platter).

9 Caravela Café
MAP M1 ■ 27, 31st January Rd,
Panaji ■ 0832 223 7448 ■ ₹₹
This quaint café serves delicious
breakfast and light eats. The menu
includes local specialities such as
rissois (shrimp patties), chorizo *pao*
(local bun), desserts and coffee.

10 Desbue
MAP M2 ■ Near St Sebastian
Chapel Fontainhas, Panaji ■ 0832
223 5555 ■ ₹₹₹
Housed in "La Maison", a beautiful
Portuguese house, this typical French
restaurant is known for its exceptional
fusion food. Enjoy European flavours
combined with traditional Goan
cuisine at its best.

See map on pp74–5 ←

TOP10 Central Goa

Wedged between the Mandovi and Zuari rivers, Central Goa captivates with its cultural richness and exuberant landscape. From impressive waterfalls and wildlife sanctuaries to medieval temples and exotic spice farms, there are a wealth of options to explore here. The temples around Ponda draw pilgrims from all over while the islands of Chorão and Divar are rich with avifauna, offering an ideal setting for birdwatchers to explore the hinterlands of Goa.

Safa Shahouri Masjid, Ponda

1 Ponda

Southeast of Panaji lies the main market town of Ponda (see pp30–31). With the Portuguese expansion in Central Goa, over 550 temples were destroyed. Hindu priests fled with religious artifacts to regions that lay outside Portuguese control, especially the area around Ponda town, where they built new temples in the 17th and 18th centuries. These temples can be found in the forests around the town and are concentrated in two main clusters – the north and in the country-side, west of the town. Another main sight here is the Safa Shahouri Masjid.

CENTRAL GOA

Top 10 Sights
see pp80–83

Places to Eat
see p85

The Best of the Rest
see p84

Goa's most impressive waterfall, Dudhsagar Falls

2 Dudhsagar Falls

Set amid spectacular scenery with a pristine tropical forest as its backdrop, this 600-m-(1,969-ft-) high waterfall *(see p32)* is the main attraction on the Goa-Karnataka border. *Dudhsagar* is a Konkani name which means "sea of milk". It is derived from the clouds of foam that rise up as the water cascades down the rocky outcrop. To reach the waterfall, visitors can either hire a four-wheel-drive jeep or take the train to Colem and then trek to the base of the falls.

3 Bhagwan Mahavir Wildlife Sanctuary

The largest of Goa's four protected areas is the Bhagwan Mahavir Wildlife Sanctuary *(see p32)*. It is located 20 km (12 miles) southeast of Tamdi Surla and covers an area of 240 sq km (93 sq miles). The sanctuary is a paradise for birdwatchers and also features the Molem National Park. Look out for the ruby-throated yellow bulbul here. Rich in wildlife, it is a good habitat for the *gaur* (Indian bison), spotted deer, hog, barking deer, leopards and elephants. The Devil's Canyon is a great viewpoint to spot wildlife. Visitors need a permit or an entry ticket to enter the sanctuary. It can be purchased at the park office.

4 Shantadurga Temple

MAP D3 ▪ Kapileswari–Kavlem Rd, Donshiwado, Ponda ▪ 0832 231 9900 ▪ www.shree shantadurga.com

About 3 km (2 miles) southwest of Ponda, at Kavlem, is the Shantadurga Temple *(see p45)*. Goa's most famous temple is dedicated to Shantadurga (also known as Santeri), who is the goddess of peace. The original temple was destroyed during the Portuguese rule, and a small mud shrine was built in its place. This was replaced by a European-inspired structure in 1730. Inside grand chandeliers hang from the gilded roof in the huge central hall. Also of interest is the golden *palkhi* (palanquin) in which the deity is carried during festive occasions.

Shantadurga Temple and the bell tower

GOAN TEMPLE ARCHITECTURE

Goan temples, unlike those elsewhere in India, are a fascinating blend of European Baroque, Islamic and Hindu architectural styles. Their basic plan remains Hindu, but often Muslim domes replace the usual *shikharas* (spires) over the main sanctum, and the prayer halls are decorated with ornate European chandeliers.

Goa Velha
MAP C3

Also known as Gopakapttana, the Goa Velha village marks the site of Govapuri, the port-capital of the Kadamba rulers between the 11th and 13th centuries, of which few traces now remain. Every year on the first Monday of Easter week, the Procession of the Saints is held, when life-sized effigies of saints, martyrs, popes and cardinals are carried around the village. The celebrations end with a mass at St Andrews Church.

Tambdi Surla Mahadev Temple

This ancient temple *(see p33)*, hidden away in the forests of Tambdi Surla, dates from the Kadamba period (between the 11th and 13th centuries). Dedicated to Mahadeva (Shiva), the temple has an entrance hall with ten pillars, and the *shikhara* (spire) above the sanctum has a miniature relief and fine carvings of Brahma, Vishnu, Shiva and his consort, Parvati.

Chorão Island
MAP L5

The picturesque island of Chorão *(see p71)* can be reached by ferry from Ribandar, which is about 5 km (3 miles) east of Panaji. It is also known as Ilha do Fidalgos or "Island of Nobelmen" after the Portuguese. The island is home to the Salim Ali Bird Sanctuary *(see p84)*, which is considered a bird-watchers paradise. Fringed by mangrove swamps, the sanctuary has flying foxes and several different species of coastal birds. The brown mudflats are also a good place to spot the bulbous-headed mudskipper.

Divar Island
MAP L5

Isolated from the mainland and accessible only by ferry from Old Goa, Divar Island *(see p71)* was once an important religious centre in pre-colonial Goa. Divar derives it name from the Konkani "dev", which translates to god, and "vaddi" to place. The two main areas on the island, Piedade and Malar, are best explored on a bike. The Church of Our Lady of Compassion occupies

Kadamba-period Tambdi Surla Temple

a hilltop in Piedade. Visitors can enjoy superb views of Old Goa from here. In August every year the feast of Bonderam *(see p68)* is celebrated here.

Bonnet macaque, Molem National Park

⑨ Molem

Located on the foothills of the Sahyadri Mountain range, this small village *(see pp32–3)* serves as the main entry point for the Bhagwan Mahavir Wildlife Sanctuary. Visitors can also access Molem National Park, which covers an area of 107 sq km (41 sq miles). The nearest railhead, Colem (Kulem) is 5 km (3 miles) south and is a drop-off point for Dudhsagar Falls.

⑩ Butterfly Conservatory of Goa

This unique conservatory *(see p31)* has been designed by Jyoti and Yashodhan Heblekar as a sanctuary for the study and conservation of butterflies. Once a barren hill slope, this area now features plenty of flora and even an artificially created stream. There's also a rainwater harvesting system. The conservatory is home to about 100 different species of colourful butterflies, but at any point in time visitors can spot up to 25 species. The best time to visit is from September to December.

A DAY IN CENTRAL GOA

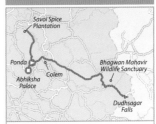

▶ MORNING

Brace yourself for a busy day packed with outdoor activities. Before you set out, it is advisable to book a taxi for the entire day. Start early as from **Ponda** *(see p80)*, it's a one-hour-long drive to the village of **Colem** *(see p33)*. From Colem hire a four-wheel-drive jeep, which will take you on a bumpy 45-minute ride through the **Bhagwan Mahavir Wildlife Sanctuary** *(see p81)* en route to the famous **Dudhsagar Falls** *(see p81)*. The drive ends with an enjoyable 15-minute hike to the base of the falls. For the adventurous, it is possible to trek to Dudhsagar as there is a 11-km (7-mile) long trail from Colem. On reaching the falls, enjoy a swim in the refreshing waters of India's second highest waterfall. Look out for monkeys that frequent the area. Remember to carry food and water as there are no shops in the vicinity of the falls. By noon, begin heading back to Colem by jeep.

AFTERNOON

From here head to the **Savoi Spice Plantation** *(see p30)* in Ponda, which is about an hour-long drive away. Take a one-hour guided tour of the 40-ha (100-acre) plantation. The cashew distillation unit here is an added attraction. The tour is followed by lunch, usually a *thali* of Goan specialities. Note that the plantation does not require advance booking and tickets can be bought on arrival. If you have the time and inclination to shop for souvenirs, head to the local market, before enjoying dinner at **Abhiksha Palace** *(see p85)* in Ponda.

See map on p80 ←

The Best of the Rest

1 Chorla Ghat
MAP E1 ▪ 50 km (31 miles) NE of Panaji ▪ Bus or car

Part of the Western Ghats, in the Sahyadri Mountain range, the Chorla Ghat (see p70) is at an elevation of 800 m (2,625 ft). It is ideal for hiking and birdwatching.

Malabar giant squirrel at Bondla's sanctuary

2 Bondla Wildlife Sanctuary
MAP E3 ▪ Khandepar Belgaum Rd, Ponda ▪ 0992 374 9287 ▪ Adm

Spot animals such as the sambar deer, Malabar giant squirrel, Indian peafowl and many more here. This sanctuary is known for its successful breeding of the *gaur* (Indian bison). There's also a lovely botanical garden and library.

3 Mahalasa Temple
The temple's (see p31) entrance porches have carvings of musicians and warriors. The most distinguishing feature here is an exceptionally tall brass pillar with 21 tiers in all.

4 Caves of Khandepar
About 4 km (2 miles) northeast of Ponda, near the village of Khandepar on the banks of the river, is a cluster of Hindu rock-cut caves (see p31). Take note of the striking lotus decorations on the ceiling.

5 Pascoal Spice Farm
MAP E3 ▪ Khandepar Belgaum Rd, Ponda ▪ 0992 374 9287 ▪ Adm

This award-winning spice farm specializes in areca, coconut and pineapple plantations. Take a guided tour of the organic farm, and round it off with a Goan buffet lunch.

6 Tropical Spice Plantation
North of Ponda, this popular plantation (see p30) organizes guided tours to show visitors how spices are produced.

7 Salim Ali Bird Sanctuary
MAP K5 ▪ Chorão Island, Ribandar ▪ 0832 222 8772 ▪ Open 6am–6pm daily ▪ Adm

Immensely popular with locals and tourists, this mangrove habitat (see p55) is also a birdwatchers paradise.

8 Safa Shahouri Masjid
Little remains of the former grandeur of Goa's oldest remaining mosque (see p31). Its exterior has a distinctive green dome, elegant Islamic arches and octagonal pillars.

9 Savoi Spice Plantation
A one-hour guided tour of this plantation (see p30) is followed by lunch, usually a *thali* of Goan specialities. Local crafts items are sold here.

10 Manguesh Temple
MAP D3 ▪ Dinanath Mangeshkar Rd, Mardol ▪ Open 6am–10pm

Goa's wealthiest temple (see p45), dedicated to Shiva, is one of the most frequently visited temples in the state. Dance-dramas are performed here during the *jatra* festivities.

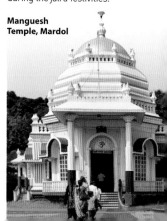

Manguesh Temple, Mardol

Places to Eat

PRICE CATEGORIES
For a meal for two, including taxes and service charge but not alcohol.

₹ under ₹700 ₹₹ ₹700–₹1500
₹₹₹ over ₹1500

1 Café Bhonsle
MAP D3 ▪ Royal Building, Kasiwada ▪ 0832 231 8725 ▪ ₹₹

Enjoy a hearty meal at Café Bhonsle, which has many branches throughout the state. This vegetarian restaurant offers a range of Goan specialities.

2 Dee Sigdii House
MAP D3 ▪ Shanti Nagar, Ponda ▪ 0832 231 8700 ▪ Closed D Mon ▪ ₹₹₹

A casual eatery with cosy wooden interiors. Fresh seafood dishes dominate the menu. The tandoori prawns are a favourite.

3 Abhiksha Palace
MAP D3 ▪ First floor, Tiska ▪ 0907 599 2827 ▪ ₹₹

This pocket-friendly restaurant in Ponda, boasts outdoor seating on its terrace. The food is delicious and the portions are generous. Try the apple chicken.

Fried pomfret with rice and vegetables

4 Lakshmi Bar & Restaurant
MAP D3 ▪ Ground floor, Central Mansion Building, Durgabhat ▪ 0832 231 4166 ▪ Closed D Sun ▪ ₹₹

This casual eatery serves the best biryani in Ponda. Good food, combined with the friendly staff, makes this place popular with both residents and visitors alike.

5 Sahakari Spice Farm
MAP D3 ▪ Ponda Belgaum Highway, Curti ▪ 0832 231 4166 ▪ Closed D ▪ ₹₹

Sample a traditional Goan lunch at this farm (see p31). Cooked in earthen pots and served on a banana leaf, the thali with Goan specialities is wholesome. Round off the meal with the local drink, feni.

6 The Rooster
MAP D3 ▪ Khadpabandh ▪ 0703 069 0989 ▪ Closed Mon & L Fri ▪ ₹₹

Famous for its biryani and grilled chicken, The Rooster is a casual dining place. The chicken popcorn or hot wings make a great snack.

7 Nature's Nest
MAP E3 ▪ Surla, Sancordem ▪ 0840 795 4664 ▪ ₹₹₹

Close to Dudhsagar Falls (see p32), this relatively remote restaurant is in a resort. Diners can enjoy mouthwatering Goan delicacies in a wonderful setting.

8 Karibu Garden
MAP F3 ▪ Collem Rd, Molem ▪ 0942 381 4466 ▪ ₹₹₹

A perfect pitstop on the way to Dudhsagar Falls (see p32), this place serves Goan specialities as well as Chinese cuisine.

9 Tilve
MAP D3 ▪ NH 17B, Donshiwado ▪ 0982 322 4545 ▪ ₹₹

A family-run restaurant, Tilve focuses on homemade traditional seafood. Enjoy the fried pomfret or the prawn fry. The menu offers plenty of vegetarian options as well.

10 Pan Aroma
MAP D3 ▪ Third floor, Padmakar Complex, Sadar ▪ 0832 231 6985 ▪ ₹₹₹

Famous for serving dishes in coconut shells, Pan Aroma is a family-friendly restaurant, offering good food and quick service. There is a separate play area for children.

See map on p80

TOP 10 North Goa

A breathtaking coastline with a series of lovely beaches, North Goa is a sunseeker's paradise. The busy strip stretching from Candolim all the way to Arambol features a string of enduringly popular places to eat, lively bars, yoga retreats, an eclectic flea market, a vibrant night bazaar and exciting watersport options. Away from the sands, fascinating museums such as the Museum of Goa and the picturesque villages of Siolim and Assagao await exploration. It's little wonder that North Goa is a firm favourite with visitors.

A Pepper Cross at MOG

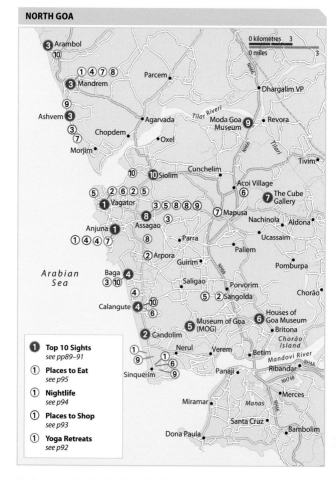

NORTH GOA

Arambol
Parcem
Mandrem
Dhargalim VP
Ashvem
Agarvada
Moda Goa Museum
Revora
Chopdem
Oxel
Morjim
Tivim
Cunchelim
Siolim
Acoi Village
Vagator
The Cube Gallery
Mapusa
Nachinola
Aldona
Anjuna
Assagao
Parra
Ucassaim
Arpora
Paliem
Guirim
Pomburpa
Arabian Sea
Baga
Saligao
Porvorim
Chorão
Calangute
Sangolda
Houses of Goa Museum
Museum of Goa (MOG)
Britona
Chorão Island
Candolim
Nerul
Verem
Betim
Mandovi River
Sinquerim
Panaji
Ribandar
Miramar
Merces
Manas
Santa Cruz
Bambolim
Dona Paula

0 kilometres 3
0 miles 3

1 Top 10 Sights
see pp89–91

1 Places to Eat
see p95

1 Nightlife
see p94

1 Places to Shop
see p93

1 Yoga Retreats
see p92

Previous pages Candolim Beach seen from Fort Aguada

Sandy Vagator Beach fringed with coconut palms

1 Vagator and Anjuna

With red stone cliffs and the ramparts of the crumbling Chapora Fort soaring above it, Vagator (see p46) is a prime stop for holiday-makers. A little towards the south is where the cove of Little Vagator (or Ozran) lies below a steep cliff, where a freshwater stream empties into a clear pool, ideal for swimming. A short distance away is Anjuna (see p47), which is sprinkled with cafés, yoga retreats, guesthouses and bars. It also offers watersports such as jetskiing and paragliding. The popular Anjuna Flea Market (see p93), held every Wednesday, is crowded with hawkers from all over India (see pp14–15).

2 Candolim

Apart from its bustling beach (see p46), which stretches right up to Fort Aguada (see p12), Candolim also features other places of interest. The highlight here is the fort, which was built in 1612 to protect the northern shores of the Mandovi from the Dutch and Maratha invaders.

Visitors can enjoy panoramic views from its four-storey Portuguese lighthouse. Candolim has numerous beach cafés. A number of popular local eateries also line the busy Fort Aguada Road.

3 Ashvem, Mandrem and Arambol

Serene Ashvem is the perfect place to enjoy a swim, indulge in fine dining and experience Goan nightlife. Mandrem and Arambol are among the many fishing villages along the northern coastline. A quiet village with a lovely beach, Mandrem is 12 km (7 miles) north of Chapora village. Nearby, Arambol, also known as Harmal, is popular with the backpacker crowd. It is situated along one of Goa's less commercial beaches. There's a sunset point on the beach, which is lively in the evenings with drum circles (see p19) and travellers practising tai chi and capoeira (see pp14–15).

4 Calangute and Baga

Both Calangute and Baga (see pp16–17) are home to the state's busiest beaches. A string of eateries and shops line both beaches. The nightlife is mainly centred around Baga and the various clubs and bars along Tito's Lane. Visitors can choose from a wide range of watersport activities that are on offer at both beaches. The lively Arpora Saturday Night Bazaar should not be missed.

Fort Aguada Lighthouse, Candolim

Exhibit at the Museum of Goa

5 Museum of Goa (MOG)

Founded by artist Subodh Kerkar *(see p43)*, this museum *(see p13)* is spread across three floors covering 1,500 sq m (16,146 sq ft). The gallery space features various art forms such as sculptures, paintings, photography, installations and moving images. Much of the art is influenced by Goa's history and interactions with the spice route. Look out for the giant sized artistic rendition of chillies. The studio as well as its landscaped surroundings serve as display areas.

6 Houses of Goa Museum

A quirky triangular-shaped structure, the Houses of Goa Museum *(see p13)*, aims to showcase Goan architectural traditions. Built by local architect Gerard da Cunha, this unique museum traces the history and impact of Portuguese influences on Goan architecture, by highlighting the changes in decor and style of residential houses.

7 The Cube Gallery

MAP K4 ■ 430/1 Calizor Vaddo, Moira ■ 0942 280 6748 ■ Open 11am–6pm Wed–Sun ■ Adm

A contemporary arts space, The Cube Gallery is based in the village of Moira. Designed by Satinder "Sonny" Singh and his wife Carolina Paez, this gallery offers a fascinating visual experience. Cubes form the basis of the gallery's architecture, and the recessed lighting and elegant landscaping make for an extraordinary spectacle at night. There's a terrace garden and a lawn with life-size sculptures.

8 Assagao

Between Mapusa and Anjuna lies sleepy Assagao *(see p15)*, which makes for a pleasant stay. This village, known for its yoga retreats, white-washed churches and Portuguese villas, is ideally located a short distance away from Goa's frenetic beachside energy, but close enough

An altar at the Houses of Goa Museum

to enjoy its excitement. Assagao's culinary reputation continues to grow with the increase in its dining options, which include outdoor restaurants.

⑨ Moda Goa Museum

MAP C2 ■ 515, St Anthony Waddo ■ 0832 242 0604 ■ Open 10am–6pm daily ■ Adm

Famous Goan fashion designer Wendell Rodricks *(see p43)* has converted his 450-year-old villa, Casa Dona Maria, in Colvale into India's first museum of fashion. This one-of-a-kind museum is dedicated to documenting and tracing the rich history and lineage of costumes in Goa. There are 15 galleries, which feature exhibits such as sculptures, paintings, illustrations, clothing, accessories, jewellery and photographs. The museum plans to introduce research rooms to feature textiles and embroideries from all over India.

A Portuguese mansion in Siolim

⑩ Siolim

One of Goa's most charming villages, Siolim *(see p15)* offers a peaceful stay due to its location inland away from the state's nearest beaches on the northern coastline. The beautiful colonial era mansions here exude an air of Portuguese prosperity. The village is home to the Corinthian Church of St Anthony, one of the oldest Christian shrines in the region. The church is known for two miracles, which were witnessed by the entire congregation in the 16th-century.

A DAY IN NORTH GOA

▶ MORNING

Begin the day with a typical English breakfast at the delightful **Café Chocolatti** *(Map J6; 409A, Fort Aguada Rd, Candolim; open 9am–7pm Mon–Sat)*. Be sure to try their brownies and Belgian-style chocolate truffles as well. Next, take a stroll to **Candolim Beach** *(see p12)* where you can simply relax under a parasol or opt for watersports such as waterskiing or parasailing. Then, make a quick trip to the **Mario Gallery** *(see p16)* to shop for Mario Miranda's sketches of Goan life, which are perfect souvenirs and keepsakes. From here take an autorickshaw to bustling Fort Aguada Road for an exceptional lunch of contemporary Burmese cuisine at **Bomra's** *(see p95)*.

AFTERNOON

Candolim Beach stretches all the way to your next stop, **Fort Aguada** *(see p12)*, which is set on a hilltop. To enjoy the views, climb to the top of the **Fort Aguada Lighthouse** *(see p12)*, which overlooks the vast expanse of sand and sea. Spend an hour here before taking a 25-minute taxi ride to Pilerne to explore the **Museum of Goa** *(see p13)*. Later in the evening, stop at **Bhatti Village Family Bar and Restaurant** *(see p59)* for authentic Goan food before taking a stroll down to **LPK Waterfront** *(see p57)* for a night of dancing. End the day by staying overnight in one of the cottages at **Aashyana Lakhanpal** *(see p116)*.

See map on p88

Yoga Retreats

1 Ashiyana Yoga Centre
This riverside tropical retreat (see p18) offers a long list of yoga courses from October to April. The on-site accommodation features heritage rooms and huts.

2 Brahmani Yoga Centre
MAP H4 ■ Tito's White House, Anjuna ■ 0937 056 8639 ■ www.brahmaniyoga.com

Established in 2003 by Julie Martin, who initiated Brahmani Yoga, this is an internationally acclaimed yoga centre. It offers drop-in yoga classes that are conducted by expert teachers.

3 Himalaya Yoga Valley
MAP G2 ■ Mandrem Beach, Junas Wadda ■ 0703 830 6467 ■ www.yogagoaindia.com

India's premier yoga education centre offers training courses for both beginners as well as seasoned practitioners.

A yoga class at Satsanga Retreat

4 Satsanga Retreat
MAP J4 ■ Naika Vado, Parra ■ 0982 213 5009 ■ www.satsangaretreat.com

This retreat describes itself as a "home away from home". It offers training as well as workshops for yoga teachers.

5 Purple Valley Centre
MAP J4 ■ H. No. 142, Bairo Alto, Assagao ■ 0832 226 8364 ■ www.yogagoa.com

A tranquil yoga shala, Purple Valley offers accommodation that ranges from simple cottages, to luxurious houses. Healthy meals are served on the terrace.

6 Yoga Magic
MAP H4 ■ 1586/1, Grand Chinvar, Anjuna ■ 0823 700 3796 ■ www.yogamagic.net

Experience Ayurvedic massages and healing therapies at this luxurious eco-friendly yoga retreat.

7 Oceanic Yoga
MAP G2 ■ Junas Wada, Mandrem Beach ■ 0904 924 7422 ■ www.oceanicyoga.com

The founder of this centre, Yogi Abhay, has meticulously fine-tuned the training courses to teach the practical and theoretical aspects of yoga.

8 Swan Yoga Retreat
MAP J4 ■ 101/4 Bairo Alto, Assagao ■ 0800 736 0677 ■ www.swan-yoga-goa.com

Set in a peaceful corner of Assagao, this retreat offers a Zen yoga experience in the satyananda and hatha tradition. Accommodation and meals are provided for week-long stays.

9 Raso Vai Ayurvedic Centre
MAP G2 ■ Wellness Inn Aswem Rd, Mandrem ■ 0962 355 6828 ■ www.rasovai.com

Several ayurvedic treatments are offered at this popular centre, especially shirodhara and pottali that are known to be deeply relaxing, energizing and rejuvenating therapies.

10 Himalayan Iyengar Yoga Centre
MAP G2 ■ Madhlo Vaddo, Arambol ■ 0981 661 1075 ■ www.hiyogacentre.com

Founded in 1985 by Anand Sagar, this centre offers a number of yoga and meditation courses, including yoga for kids.

See map on p88

Places to Shop

Colourful items at Anjuna Flea Market

1 Anjuna Flea Market
A riot of colours, stalls and goods greet shoppers at this overwhelmingly popular market *(see p15)*.

2 Arpora Saturday Night Bazaar
MAP H4 ▪ Aguada–Siolim Rd, Arpora ▪ Open Nov–Mar: 6pm–midnight Sat ▪ www.snmgoa.com

Shop for trinkets, sample local food and enjoy live music at this fun night bazaar *(see p62)*.

3 Le Souk by Amarya
MAP G3 ▪ Ashvem Beach (behind La Plage) ▪ Open daily ▪ www.amaryagroup.com/lezouk-amarya

Goa's first luxury market *(see p62)* is open every day. It focuses on clothing by top national and international designers.

4 Artjuna
MAP H4 ▪ 972 Market Rd, Monteiro Vaddo, Anjuna ▪ Open 8am–7:30pm daily

This trendy boutique *(see p63)* has a Mediterranean café. It stocks women's clothing, accessories and homeware.

5 People Tree
MAP J4 ▪ Villa No. 6, Saunta Vaddo, Assagao ▪ Open 11am–11pm Tue–Sun ▪ www.peopletreeonline.com

Set in quiet Assagao, this art and design studio *(see p63)* specializes in handcrafted clothing and accessories.

Cosy interior of Paper Boat Collective

6 The Attic
MAP J4 ▪ H. No. 69, near Mount Carmel Chapel Camarcazana, Mapusa ▪ Open 10am–7pm Mon–Sat

A stylish, contemporary gallery, The Attic *(see p63)* features exquisite vintage furniture and intricate glassware.

7 Mapusa Market
Vibrant and bustling, Mapusa's market *(see p15)* offers antiques, handicrafts, textiles and spices. Bargain hard for the best price.

8 Cheshire Cat Gallery
MAP J4 ▪ H. No. 136, Bairro Alto, Assagao ▪ 0982 258 0898 ▪ Open 10am–6pm daily

Housed in a beautifully restored Portuguese villa, this store owned by Kees van Andel and Karen Peace features an eclectic collection of jewellery, fashion and art. It also offers prints by local and international designers.

9 Literati
Set in the midst of a large garden is a treasure trove of books. This 100-year old bookshop *(see p17)* has a lovely reading room and a café.

10 Paper Boat Collective
MAP J5 ▪ 248, Bella Vista, Chogm Rd, Sangolda ▪ Open 10:30am–7:30pm Mon–Sat

This concept store *(see p62)* is an ideal place to shop for latest items exclusively created by Indian designers.

Nightlife

1 Showbar Exchange
MAP G6 ■ Beside SinQ Nightclub, Sinquerim, Candolim ■ 0880 500 2432 ■ Open 7pm–1am Wed & Sat–Mon (until 3am Thu, Fri & Tue)

This vintage retro pub follows the concept of a liquor stock exchange where prices for alcohol fluctuate according to demand.

2 Hill Top
MAP H4 ■ Ozran Beach Rd, Vagator ■ 0703 806 6665 ■ Open winters only: Nov–Mar ■ www.hilltopgoa.in

Goa's iconic party destination, Hill Top (see p56) attracts visitors from across the globe.

3 Club Tito's
MAP H5 ■ Titos Lane, Baga ■ Open 9am–3am Tue–Sun ■ www.titosgoa.com

One of the first clubs to open in Goa, this spot (see p56) has achieved legendary status.

4 Shiva Valley
MAP H4 ■ Anjuna Beach, near Anjuna Flea Market ■ 0968 962 8008 ■ Open 9am–11pm daily

Known for its psychedelic parties, Shiva Valley (see p57) is popular for its cutting-edge music.

5 Chronicle
MAP H4 ■ Little Vagator ■ 0982 321 2607

Set on a clifftop, Chronicle (see p57) has an outdoor dance floor. There's a cocktail bar and lounge as well.

6 Sinq Night Club
MAP H5 ■ Opposite Taj Holiday Village, Aguada Rd, Candolim ■ Open 10pm–3am daily ■ www.sinq.in

An upbeat and trendy club (see p56) which offers great entertainment.

7 SOMA Project
MAP J3 ■ Plot No. 301/1, Siolim ■ 0982 239 5522 ■ Open 11am–11pm Mon–Sat, noon–12am Sun

Set in the most isolated part of Ashvem Beach (see pp56–7), this nightspot can rival the beach clubs of Ibiza.

8 Club Cubana
MAP H4 ■ Calangute–Arpora Rd, Arpora ■ 0982 353 9000 ■ www.clubcubanagoa.com

This neon-lit nightclub (see p56) hosts some of the most happening parties.

9 Cohiba
MAP J6 ■ Aguada–Siolim Rd, Aguada Fort Area, Candolim ■ 0772 203 1222 ■ Open 6pm–2am daily

Close to the Aguada Fort Lighthouse (see p12), this club has a welcoming vibe. The foot-stomping music is great.

10 Cape Town Café
MAP H5 ■ Tito's Lane, Baga Calangute Rd ■ 0992 332 5638 ■ Open 6pm–4am daily

Hosting international DJs, this place entertains its guests well. Watch live sporting events on its LCD screens.

Chronicle at sunset

Places To Eat

Outdoor seating at Bomra's

PRICE CATEGORIES

For a meal for two, including taxes and service charge but not alcohol.

₹ under ₹700   ₹₹ ₹700–₹1500
₹₹₹ over ₹1500

1 Bomra's
MAP H5 ■ Souza Vaddo, Candolim ■ 0976 759 1056 ■ ₹₹₹

This award-winning Burmese restaurant (see p60) is known for its mouthwatering fare.

2 Morgan's Place
MAP J5 ■ 66, Chogm Rd, Sangolda ■ 0988 666 6750 ■ ₹₹

The menu at this Alice In Wonderland themed restaurant has a mix of everything from Italian delicacies to German delights.

3 Sublime
MAP H3 ■ Morjim Beach Rd, Vithaldas Vaddo, Morjim ■ 0982 248 4051 ■ Closed Mon ■ ₹₹₹

A picturesque beachside restaurant, Sublime (see p60) offers a blend of Asian and Goan cuisine.

4 A Reverie
MAP H5 ■ Holiday St, Gaura Waddo, Calangute ■ 982 317 4927 ■ Closed L ■ ₹₹₹

This gourmet restaurant (see p60) offers innovative cooking alongside an extravagant ambience. The menu features an extensive wine list.

5 Sakana
MAP H4 ■ Chapora Rd, Anjuna ■ 0989 013 5502 ■ ₹₹₹

Known for their hearty breakfasts, Sakana (see p60) offers fresh croissants and baked apple pie.

6 Infantaria
MAP H5 ■ 5/181, Calangute Baga Junction ■ 0992 220 2526 ■ ₹₹

With a nostalgic air, Infantaria (see p61) has a menu offering perfect breakfasts. Try their desserts.

7 Baba Au Rhum
MAP H4 ■ 1054, Sim Vaddo, Anjuna ■ 0982 286 6366 ■ Closed Tue D ■ ₹₹

With an eco friendly decor, this cosy café-bakery (see p61) serves excellent teas and Vietnamese coffees.

Almond croissant, Baba Au Rhum

8 Café Nu
MAP J1 ■ 182, Junos Vaddo, Pernem ■ 0985 065 8568 ■ ₹₹₹

Charming restaurant (see p61) located in a pretty garden offers light gourmet bites.

9 Calamari
MAP J6 ■ Dando Beach, Candolim ■ 0735 007 5105 ■ ₹₹₹

Serving the best calamari in Goa, this beachfront restaurant also has live music. The seafood options are great.

10 Thalassa
MAP H4 ■ Little Vagator, Orzan ■ 0985 003 3537 ■ ₹₹₹

With outdoor tables shaded by palm trees, Thalassa (see p60) offers authentic Greek cuisine as well as picturesque views of the sea.

See map on p88 ←

TOP 10 South Goa

Goa's idyllic south coast caters to a growing number of visitors every year. Fringed by some of the region's finest beaches such as Palolem, Agonda and Colva, South Goa's coastline is still more sedate when compared to the bustling beaches on the northern strip. Margao is the state's second city after Panaji, and is the main market town. The little hidden gem Bogmalo is a perfect base for exploring the southern stretch. Inland, the villages of Chandor and Loutolim are scattered with a cluster of sumptuous Portuguese-era mansions, including the delightful 300-year old Braganza House. Further east from Margao is Rachol, which is renowned as the site of a 16th-century Jewish seminary. In the far south, the Cotigao Wildlife Sanctuary is a paradise for birds and offers a rare glimpse of rich flora.

Bust at the Municipal Garden, Margao

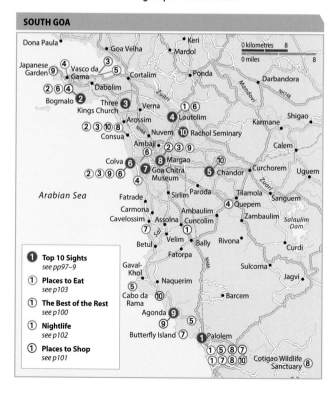

SOUTH GOA

Dona Paula • • Keri
• Goa Velha • Mardol
0 kilometres   8
0 miles   8

Japanese Garden ⑨ ④ Vasco da ③ Cortalim • Ponda • Darbandora
Gama ⑤
②⑥④ Dabolim Zuari NH748
Bogmalo ② Three ③ Verna ①⑥ Shigao
Kings Church Arossim ④ Loutolim Karmane
②③⑩⑧ NH66 Nuvem ⑩ Rachol Seminary Calem
Consua Ambaji ②③⑨
⑥ ⑧ Margao ⑩
Colva ⑥ ⑦ Goa Chitra ⑤ Chandor • Curchorem Uguem
②③⑨⑥ Museum Zuari
④ Fatrade • Sirlim Paroda Tilamola • Sanguem
Carmona ④ Quepem Zambaulim Salaulim
Cavelossim • Assolna Cuncolim Dam
⑦ Sol Velim • Bally Rivona • Curdi
Betul • Fatorpa

Arabian Sea

Gaval-Khol Sulcorna •
⑤ • Naquerim Jagvi
Cabo da ⑩
Rama • Barcem
Agonda ⑨
⑨ ⑤
Butterfly Island ⑦ ① Palolem
①⑤⑧⑦
①⑦⑧⑩ Cotigao Wildlife ⑧
Sanctuary

① **Top 10 Sights**
see pp97–9

① **Places to Eat**
see p103

① **The Best of the Rest**
see p100

① **Nightlife**
see p102

① **Places to Shop**
see p101

Colourful wooden beach huts, Palolem

1 Palolem
MAP D6

Charming Palolem's (see pp38–9) remote location, away from the crowded beaches of Central Goa, makes it ideal for a quiet holiday. The beach (see p48) stretches on for miles, and is lined with coco-nut palms, shacks and Thai-style camping huts. The restaurants here are stylish and the nightlife is dominated by the weekly head-phone parties, which circumvent the ban on amplified music after 10pm in Goa.

2 Bogmalo
MAP C3

Once a quiet fishing village, Bogmalo (see p49) is now a busy town, close to one of India's busiest naval bases and Dabolim Airport. The beach is clean and is usually not too crowded. Head to the many bars and shacks along the beach for a break and for live music. The vicinity is also packed with sights such as the fascinating Naval Aviation Museum (see p100).

3 Three Kings Church
MAP C3 ■ Muder, Cansaulim

North of Cansaulim, perched atop a hill in Cuelim, is the Church of Our Lady of Remedios, commonly known as the Three Kings Church. It is believed to be haunted and harks back to the legend of three Portuguese kings, one of whom plotted to poison the others, but died himself in the process. All three were buried inside the church and ever since then, locals claim to have sighted ghostly apparitions here. The small church is famous for the Three Kings Feast (see p68) celebrated in January every year. During the feast, three young boys are chosen from any of the neighbouring villages to represent the three kings. The celebrations also include a colourful fair, which is held on the grounds of the church. Visitors can enjoy lovely views of the surrounding areas from here.

4 Loutolim
MAP B4

Picturesque Loutolim features several remnants of Goa's fine Portuguese heritage. In the heart of the village lies the majestic 16th-century Church of Salvador do Mundo (Saviour of the World). Nearby is Ancestral Goa (see p35), which offers a unique glimpse into traditional trades and crafts from over a hundred years ago. The village is also home to many impressive stately homes, including the historic 500-year old Figueiredo Mansion (see p34) and Casa Araujo Alvares.

Ancestral Goa in Loutolim

Antique furniture in the charming Braganza House, Chandor

5 Chandor
MAP D4

About 13 km (8 miles) east of Margao is the sleepy village of Chandor. Between the 6th and 11th centuries, Chandor, then known as Chandrapur, was the capital of the Kadamba dynasty. It remained the capital until 1054 when the Kadambas moved to Govapuri, now known as Goa Velha (see p82). However, the Muslim invasion in 1312 forced the Kadambas to move back to Chandrapur, but only for a brief period as the Portuguese invaded the city in 1327. Today, the main attraction here is Braganza House (see p100), which is regarded as the grandest of Goa's colonial mansions.

6 Colva
Known for its powder-white sands, Colva's (see p48) 25-km (16-mile) long sandy beach draws vast numbers of visitors, who spend the day enjoying the lively atmosphere of its many beach shacks, which serve delicious seafood specialities. Hotels and guesthouses line the main beach road, while the southern end features more pristine stretches. Standing a short distance from the sea is Colva's Church of Our Lady of Mercy, built in 1630. The church has an attractive Baroque interior and houses the famous statue of Menino (baby) Jesus, holding an orb and a flag, revered for its miraculous healing powers.

7 Goa Chitra Museum
With over 4,000 artifacts on display, this splendid ethnographic museum (see p35) is highly regarded by the Archaeological Survey of India (ASI). Founded by artist-turned-curator Victor Hugo Gomes, the museum showcases a unique collection of antique agricultural tools set up against the backdrop of a traditional organic farm. A unique aspect is its use of traditional recycling techniques. The museum is also home to the Goa Chakra museum, which displays ancient modes of transportation in India and Goa Cruti's collection, which features exhibits based on the state's colonial past.

8 Margao
A commercial hub, the bustling town of Margao (see pp34–5) serves as the area's main trading centre. The town square features the colonial Municipal Building, which houses an impressive library on its southern side.

THE VASCO SAPTAH
One of the biggest festivals in Goa, the Vasco Saptah has been a Goan tradition since 1898. It is said that during an epidemic, the locals visited the Zambaulim temple in Margao and brought back a coconut to Vasco. Soon after, a miracle occurred and the plague ended. The festival is now celebrated every year for seven days in August.

Just behind the building, to the south, are Margao's lively bazaars, selling the day's catch of fish. Its central square, Largo de Igreja, is surrounded by colourful 18th- and 19th-century town houses. In the centre of the square is a monumental,16th-century cross, overlooked by the Church of the Holy Spirit (see p34). Nearby is the unique Sat Burnzam Ghor (see p35) mansion.

9 Agonda

With relatively few visitors, this pristine beach (see p38) makes for a great spot to sunbathe. The sea is slightly rough here, so the waters may not always be ideal for a swim. At the northern end of the beach is the nesting site of the protected Olive Ridley turtles. Away from the beach, visitors can opt for yoga, meditation and Ayurveda classes. There are also a number of reliable operators offering dolphin-spotting trips.

10 Rachol Seminary

Built in 1606, the Rachol Seminary (see p35) is probably the most important of Goa's seminaries. For generations, this was Goa's most prestigious educational institution, both for secular and religious studies. The entrance is covered with impressive murals and opens on to a central courtyard. The grand staircase, adorned with Hindu sculptures, leads to the library, which has a rare collection of Latin and Portuguese books. Attached to the seminary is the Church of St Ignatius Loyola, which has a beautiful 16th-century pipe-organ from Lisbon.

Façade of the Rachol Seminary

A DAY IN SOUTH GOA

Loutolim
Ancestral Goa
Margao
Chandor, Braganza House
Palácio do Deão
Palolem Beach, Ourem 88, Silent Noise

▶ MORNING

Spend the day admiring the colonial architecture of the historic Portuguese-era mansions scattered inland from **Margao**. Head to the fascinating **Ancestral Goa** (see p35) in **Loutolim** (see p97), also known as Big Foot Museum, a model village with life-size statues of craftsmen depicting early Goan village life. Next, drive 13 km (8 miles) east of Margao, to sleepy **Chandor** to explore one of Goa's grandest colonial mansions, **Braganza House** (see p34). The house built in the 1500s has a huge double storey façade with 28 windows flanking its entrance. A 30-minute drive southeast of Margao will lead you to Quepem, where you can stop for lunch at the superb **Palácio do Deão** (see p35), a 200-year old Indo-Portuguese mansion. Enjoy a Goan meal on the terrace overlooking the river.

AFTERNOON

Next, head to **Palolem Beach** (see p48), which is one of South Goa's most famous beaches. Lined with coconut palms, its clear waters are perfect for kayaking and stand-up paddle-boarding. Scuba diving is offered by Shanti Divers (www.shanti divers.com). In the evening, head to **Ourem 88** (see p103) for a sumptuous meal. Enjoy European gastro dishes made from fresh local ingredients here. After dinner make your way to **Silent Noise** (see p102), located on a rock promontory at the southern end of the bay. Headphone parties are held here on Saturday nights.

See map on p96

The Best of the Rest

1 Figueiredo Mansion
This 16th-century mansion *(see p34)* in Loutolim is older than the Taj Mahal. It is a fine combination of Indian and Portuguese architecture.

2 Naval Aviation Museum
MAP C3 ▪ Bogmalo Rd, Vasco da Gama ▪ Open 10am–5pm Tue–Sun ▪ Adm (additional charge for photography) ▪ www.navalaviation museumgoa.com

A unique military museum *(see p55)* which displays the evolution of the Indian Naval Aviation. It exhibits rare and old aircrafts and torpedoes.

3 Sao Jacinto and Sao Antonio Islands
MAP C3

These two islands are dotted with traditional houses. Highlights are an old Portuguese lighthouse and the St Hyacinth Church.

Exotic Butterfly

4 Palácio do Deão
This 213-year-old mansion *(see p35)* was built by a Portuguese church dean. Lush with gardens, it continues to preserve its history.

5 Cabo da Rama
This fort *(see p39)* belonged to various rulers until 1763, when it was occupied by the Portuguese. The observation post offers great views.

6 Ancestral Goa
Visit Ancestral Goa *(see p35)* to experience Goan rural life from the past century. It houses the Big Foot Museum as well as a mammoth sculpture of Mirabai *(see p55)*.

7 Butterfly Beach
North of Patnem and Palolem Beach lies the beautiful and uninhabited Butterfly Beach *(see p38)*, which is only accessible by boat. It is a great dolphin-spotting place. Carry food and drink as there are no eateries here.

8 Cotigao Wildlife Sanctuary
This scenic sanctuary *(see p39)* makes for a pleasant day-trip from Palolem. It is best visited between October and March.

9 Japanese Garden
MAP C3 ▪ Marmugao Port, Vasco da Gama ▪ Open 5am–8pm daily

Soak in the magnificent views of the Zuari River and the Arabian Sea, while admiring the ruins of the Fortaleza Santa Catarina from this well-kept garden.

10 Braganza House
The biggest Portuguese mansion *(see p34)* of its kind, this 17th-century house is a unique example of Portuguese architecture.

Breathtaking views from the Cabo da Rama fort

Places to Shop

1 Prakash Chitari
MAP D5 ■ 2499, Demani Wada, Cuncolim ■ 0982 298 6793 ■ Open 8:30am–noon, 2–6pm daily

Ask for directions from Cuncolim market to reach this workshop, known for its ornately painted and lacquered wooden carvings. Though the stock is limited, you may find *advolis* (cutting boards) or a *puja* (prayer) table or stool.

2 Margao Municipal Market
MAP B5 ■ Open 9am–2pm & 4–8pm daily

The shops here sell a variety of items as well as Goan spices such as cinnamon, cardamom, *trifala* or *teflam* (Sichuan spices) and *dagadful* (black stone flower).

3 Tuk Tuk
MAP B5 ■ 1st floor, Pereira Plaza, Margao ■ 0904 901 7182 ■ Open 10am–7pm Mon–Sat

With two stores, one in Margao and the other in Benaulim, Tuk Tuk is popular for souvenirs. Shop for quirky items such as handcrafted baskets, jewellery, clothes and trinkets here.

4 Zanskar Arts
MAP C3 ■ Bogmalo Beach Rd ■ 0832 253 8253 ■ Open 9am–10pm daily

Find items ranging from pashminas and jewellery to gifts and trinkets here. You can also buy traditional souvenirs at this one-stop shop.

5 La Mangrove Boutique
MAP D6

Associated with a luxury resort of the same name, this bohemian-themed store offers beach- and lounge-wear.

6 Colva Beach Market
MAP A5

Attracting an international crowd, the Colva Beach Market offers a distinct and colourful shopping experience. Here you can shop for local items at negotiable prices.

Designer clothing at Chim

7 Chim
MAP D6 ■ Palolem Beach Rd, Canacona ■ 0832 264 3144 ■ Open 9am–10pm daily

Set on the beach, this store has objects ranging from designer clothing to local craft items.

8 Jaali Boutique
MAP D6 ■ Patnem Rd, Palolem, ■ 0800 771 2248 ■ Open 9am–6pm Tue, Wed & Sun (until 10pm Thu–Sat)

Located in a shady tropical garden, this store sells typical Rajasthani jewellery as well as several vintage one-of-a-kind souvenirs.

9 Augustin Studio and Gallery
MAP D5 ■ Opposite the church, Agonda Beach ■ 0706 629 3608

Those interested in art must visit this gallery for its art collection. The displayed artworks can be purchased at reasonable prices.

10 Miss Monkey
MAP D5 ■ 124 Parvem, Agonda ■ 0916 824 8340 ■ Open 11am–1pm & 5–9pm daily

This high-end clothing store offers some unique designs sporting a bohemian style. The clothes are made with natural fibres.

See map on p96

Nightlife

1 Sundowner
MAP D6 ▪ Hira Smruti, Sawant Wade, Palolem ▪ 0788 756 7384

This open-air bar is a great spot to enjoy a drink and the sweeping bay views. There's a good range of cocktails and small bites.

Well-lit bar at Sundowner

2 Edge
MAP A5 ▪ 48/10 Alila Diwa Goa Village, Majorda ▪ 0832 274 6800 ▪ Open 9am–7pm daily

Setting the pace of the city's nightlife, Edge offers a unique experience. A pool bar by day, it transforms into a hip lounge in the evening. Try the amazing cocktails.

3 Lorry Back Bar
MAP A5 ▪ Costa Vaddo, Majorda ▪ 0832 322 1119 ▪ www.vivendagoa. com

Located in a restored Portuguese house, this bar is actually a converted lorry. The painted back of the truck forms the bar's shutter. It is an ideal place to enjoy a drink.

4 Adega Camoens
MAP A6 ▪ Taj Exotica, Calwaddo ▪ 0832 668 3333

Elegant black-and-white photos of Hollywood film celebrities adorn the line panels at this nightspot. The music enhances its old-world charm, making it perfect for a romantic evening over cocktails and cognac.

5 Leopard Valley
MAP D6 ▪ Agonda Rd, Palolem ▪ Open 10am–6pm Mon, Wed, Thu, Sat & Sun, 9pm–3am Tue & Fri ▪ Closed mid-May–Oct ▪ www. leopardvalley.com

This high-octane nightclub (see p57) is set in a jungle quarry. It features a 7-m (23-ft) high DJ stage.

6 Red Ginger
MAP A5 ▪ Florida Garden, Colva Rd, Margao ▪ 0888 847 6666 ▪ Open 11am–11:30pm Mon & Thu–Sat (from noon Tue, Wed & Sun)

The stunning bar, great ambience and fabulous music makes this a great nightspot.

7 Neptune's Point
MAP D6 ▪ Palolem Beach ▪ 0915 843 2629

With a dreamy beach location, Neptune's Point is the place to groove to techno and trance beats.

8 Silent Noise
MAP D6 ▪ Palolem ▪ 0928 479 1484 ▪ Open 7pm–2am Mon–Wed, Fri & Sun, 7pm–midnight Thu & Sat, midnight–2pm Fri & Sun ▪ www. silentnoise.in

Revellers are provided with wireless headsets here (see p57) that allow them to switch between each of the three DJs playing.

9 Club Margarita
MAP A5 ▪ Colva Beach Rd ▪ 0976 701 6858 ▪ Open 8pm–2am daily

A popular hangout near Colva Beach, this welcoming place offers good entertainment.

10 Cleopatra's
MAP D6 ▪ Palolem, Canacona ▪ 0983 4992 259 ▪ Open 9am–11:30pm daily

If you're out late, this quiet restaurant-bar is a perfect spot to dine. The prices tend to go up if you wish to dine later.

Places To Eat

PRICE CATEGORIES
For a meal for two, including taxes and
service charge but not alcohol.

₹ under ₹700 ₹₹ ₹700–₹1500
₹₹₹ over ₹1500

① Ourem 88
MAP D6 ▪ South end of
Palolem Beach, behind Rococo Pelton
▪ 0869 882 7679 ▪ Closed L ▪ ₹₹₹

This quaint restaurant (see p61) has
cosy interiors. Enjoy the music as
you dig into the delicious food.

② Leda
MAP A5 ▪ Colva Beach Rd
▪ 0832 278 1458 ▪ ₹₹₹

Savour the sizzlers and salmon as
well as the Indian tandoori dishes
that are offered here.

③ Mickey's
MAP A5 ▪ Near Bollywood Resort,
Colva Beach ▪ 0832 278 9125 ▪ ₹₹₹

Enjoy live music in the evenings
here. Try their signature cheese
and sausage naan (bread).

④ Anantashram
MAP C3 ▪ Father Jose Vaz Rd,
Vasco da Gama ▪ 0774 481 8888
▪ Closed Sun ▪ ₹₹₹

Relish the traditional flavours at this
local eatery. The Goan thali is delicious.

Striking interior of Anantashram

⑤ Sheela Bar and Restaurant
MAP C3 ▪ NH 17A, Vidhyanagar
Colony, Vasco da Gama ▪ 0832 255
5675 ▪ Closed Mon ▪ ₹₹₹

Off-beat yet in an accessible location,
Sheela Bar includes Goan favourites
such as fish and prawn curries.

⑥ Joet's Bar and Restaurant
MAP C3 ▪ Bogmalo Beach,
Vasco da Gama ▪ 0832 278 9125 ▪ ₹₹₹

This perfectly located beach shack has
the best view of Bogmalo Beach (see
p97). There is live music every Friday.

⑦ Robin's Ark
MAP D5 ▪ Luisa By the Sea
Complex, Mobor Beach ▪ 0884 777
8388 ▪ ₹₹₹

A multi-cuisine restaurant with a
wonderful location and an appetizing
menu. Try their beef chilly, prawn
curry and fish fry.

⑧ FishKa
MAP A5 ▪ Opposite Hotel Alila
Diwa Goa, Betalbatim ▪ 0963 737
9228 ▪ ₹₹

Conveniently located, this is a
popular spot for drinks and seafood.
The menu here is reasonably priced.

⑨ Longhuino's
MAP B5 ▪ Ground floor,
Dr Antonio Dias Building, Margao
▪ 0832 273 9908 ▪ ₹₹₹

Set in the heart of
Margao, this place has
maintained its vintage
charm. The sausage and
fish thali are favourites.

⑩ Pentagon
MAP A5
▪ Majorda Beach Rd
▪ 0832 288 1402 ▪ ₹₹₹

With a rustic charm,
this restaurant offers
sunset views. There is
live entertainment in
the evenings. Try their
tandoori dishes.

See map on p96

Top 10 Goa
Streetsmart

**Sunset at a typical Goan beach shack
fringed by shady palm trees**

Getting To and Around Goa

Arriving by Air

Goa International Airport, also known as Dabolim Airport, handles domestic as well as international flights. Domestic flight carriers include **Air India**, **AirAsia India**, **IndiGo**, **GoAir**, **SpiceJet** and **Vistara**. There are also direct international flights to Goa from major hubs in the Middle East – Kuwait, Oman, Qatar, Dubai – and from London. **Gulf Air**, **Etihad Airways**, **Qatar Airways**, **British Airways**, **Oman Air** and **Lufthansa** are the international flight carriers.

Goa's airport is located 4 km (3 miles) from Vasco da Gama, 27 km (17 miles) from Panaji and 38 km (24 miles) from Calangute. The best option to travel into town from the airport is to take a taxi. There are many pre-paid taxi kiosks outside the terminal, but prices may vary based on distance.

There are local buses outside the airport, which head to Vasco da Gama, but they are often uncomfortable, especially if you're carrying luggage. In case you are staying at a good hotel check if they provide an airport pickup or have a shuttle service from the airport.

Arriving by Train

There are two main railway stations in the southern part of Goa – in Margao and Vasco da Gama. The Madgaon (Margao) station is the largest railway junction in Goa. It's the terminal for the Konkan Railway which runs high-speed trains between Mumbai and Goa. A journey from Mumbai usually takes about 10 to 13 hours.

The South Central Railway operates all its trains from the Vasco da Gama terminal. The Nizamuddin Goa Express (Delhi–Goa) also runs from this station, as do trains linking Karnataka. It is advisable to keep an eye on your baggage at the station.

You can book your train at the railway station or at the **Konkan Railway Reservation Office**, which is located at Kadamba Bus Stand. Tickets can also be booked online through the **Indian Railways Catering and Tourism Corporation (IRCTC)**. Check the **Indian Railways** website for train schedules, or call **Railway Enquiries** if you have any questions.

It is easy to travel to the city from the station as rail terminals have kiosks for pre-paid taxis, as well as auto-rickshaw services.

Arriving by Road

There are two National Highways that lead into the state, NH 66 links Goa to the north and the south, while NH 748 leads to the east. These highways also connect Goa to Mumbai, which is around 587 km (365 miles) away.

It is advisable to travel by bus if you wish to save on expenses. The state's main bus station is the **Kadamba Bus Stand**, which is 10 km (6 miles) from the Madgaon railway station. The **Mapusa Bus Stand** is a major transport hub for those visiting the beaches of north Goa. Fares vary depending on the route, distance and the type of bus that you are travelling in. A bus journey from Mumbai would take about 12 to 16 hours.

Travelling by Motorbike or Moped

Bike rides in Goa are a highlight for bikers. Bike rentals are available in every corner and Panaji has numerous bike rental shops. However, you could also ask your hotel or a local where to rent a bike from. To rent a bike, you will need to submit your driving license or any valid photo ID as collateral. Make sure to collect all bike documents from the dealer. It is also important to test that the bike is in working order. It is wise to take pictures of your bike before renting it so that you aren't charged for any damage that you aren't responsible for.

Travelling by Taxi

You should know how much you need to pay before you hail a taxi as you may have to haggle for the fare. Check with your hotel as they should be able to book you a cab. There are also many private car rental companies that offer cars for hire to make your travel easier. Visitors can book a taxi from either **Goa Cabs**, **GoanTaxi**, **Savaari**, **TaxiGo** and **TraveloCar** online, by phone, or via their apps.

Travelling by Auto-Rickshaw

Auto-rickshaws or "autos" are the standard way of getting around Goa. They are fitted with meters, but most drivers won't use them and you will probably have to haggle. Know what price you should pay before stopping an auto, and agree to a fare before setting off. Fares should be ₹19 for the first kilometre then roughly ₹6.50 per kilometre. You can avoid having to haggle (and ensure you don't get overcharged) by hiring pre-paid autos at official set rates from kiosks at major transport terminals.

Travelling by Motorcycle Rickshaw

Motorcycle rickshaws are the cheapest way to get around the city, with fares that can be negotiated. These vehicles are driven by drivers who are locally called "pilots". They can carry a single rider.

Travelling by Bus

The city has an extensive bus network. There are two kinds of buses – the locals, that halt at every stop, and the shuttles that travel to all the important sights. Fares range from ₹10–40 and the buses run from 7am to 7pm.

Travelling by Train

It is better to use a local train in order to travel to far off places. For example, it is a good idea to take a train from Mapusa to Palolem, otherwise you will have to change between many buses.

Travelling by Ferry

Boats and ferries are an age-old transport in Goa and are still an important means of commuting. Travelling by ferry is the fastest way to commute from the mainland to the islands. It is also the best way to experience Goa's culture in the rural areas.

DIRECTORY

ARRIVING BY AIR

AirAsia India
📞 1 804 666 2222
🌐 airasia.com

Air India
📞 1 800 180 1407
🌐 airindia.in

British Airways
📞 0124 417 3777
🌐 britishairways.com

Etihad Airways
📞 1 800 209 0808
🌐 etihad.com

GoAir
📞 0922 322 2111
🌐 goair.in

Goa International Airport
📞 0832 254 0806

Gulf Air
📞 0484 402 9190
🌐 gulfair.com

IndiGo
📞 0921 278 3838
🌐 goindigo.in

Lufthansa
📞 1 800 102 5838
🌐 lufthansa.com

Oman Air
📞 0793 061 6000
🌐 omanair.com

Qatar Airways
📞 0793 061 6000
🌐 qatarairways.com

SpiceJet
📞 0987 180 3333
🌐 spicejet.com

Vistara
📞 0928 922 8888
🌐 airvistara.com

ARRIVING BY TRAIN

Indian Railways
🌐 indianrail.gov.in

Indian Railways Catering and Tourism Corporation (IRCTC)
🌐 irctc.co.in

Konkan Railway Reservation Office
Kadamba Bus Stand, First Floor
📞 0960 462 9761

Railway Enquiries
📞 139
🌐 enquiry.indianrail.gov.in/ntes

ARRIVING BY ROAD

Kadamba Bus Stand
📞 0832 243 8035

Mapusa Bus Stand
📞 0832 223 2161

TRAVELLING BY TAXI

Goa Cabs
📞 0986 012 2226
🌐 goacabs.com

GoanTaxi
📞 0986 085 5521
🌐 goantaxi.com

Savaari
📞 0904 545 0000
🌐 savaari.com

TaxiGo
📞 0832 671 1111
🌐 taxigo.co.in

TraveloCar
📞 0793 368 5555
🌐 travelocar.com

Practical Information

Passports and Visas

Everyone (except citizens of Nepal and Bhutan) needs a visa to enter India. Nationals of most countries, if arriving at Goa airport with an onward or return ticket, can get a 30-day tourist visa online before their departure. For a longer stay, you need to apply in person or by post at a Visa Office or alternatively at the Indian Embassy or High Commission in your home country. For details, check the **Ministry of External Affairs** website.

The Indian government has introduced e-Tourist Visa, which allows foreign travellers to visit India without going through the tiresome process of going to the embassy and waiting for its approval. You can apply through an online portal, four days before the expected date of travel. It is best to allow plenty of time though. This visa is valid for 30 days, and costs US$60 per passenger. Be sure to apply through the official website. There are numerous scam sites, so beware of giving away personal information to third party agents.

Your passport should be valid for at least six months beyond your arrival date. The **UK**, **US**, **Canada**, **Australia**, **New Zealand** and many other countries have consular representation in the city.

Customs and Immigration

Duty-free limits are 2 litres of liquor and 200 cigarettes or 50 cigars or 250 g (9 oz) tobacco. You must also fill a currency declaration form if the aggregate value of your foreign currency (bank notes and travellers cheques) is more than US$10,000 or equivalent.

Travel Safety Advice

Visitors can get up-to-date travel safety information from the **UK Foreign and Commonwealth Office**, the **US Department of State** and the **Australian Department of Foreign Affairs and Trade**.

Travel Insurance

Don't travel without valid insurance, and check the details of the policy, particularly how much you can claim for the loss of individual items. For medical treatment you may have to pay upfront and claim it later.

Health

Vaccinations against meningitis, typhoid, tetanus as well as hepatitis A are commonly recommended for India. Make sure that you are covered against polio. Consult your doctor before your trip regarding the exact requirements. Malaria and dengue fever outbreaks can occur, especially in and after the monsoon months (June–September), so bring high-DEET repellent and protect yourself against mosquito bites.

Stick to bottled drinking water (or purify your own) and avoid street food as it can play havoc with those who have delicate constitutions. The most common tourist illness is stomach upset that passes within a day or two (stick to water, yoghurt and rice). If your symptoms persist, it's a good idea to consult a doctor in case it's giardia or amoebic dysentery. **Manipal Health Systems Pvt Ltd** is one of the top research hospitals; other hospitals include the **Vintage Hospital & Medical Research Centre Pvt Ltd**, **Dr Kolwalkar's Galaxy Hospital** and the **Apollo Victor Hospital**. The **Wellness Forever** pharmacy in Panaji is open 24x7.

Personal Security

Cases of petty theft such as pickpocketing and pilfering from hotel rooms are quite common, as is credit card fraud. If you are paying with credit or debit cards, ensure that it is swiped in front of you. Most hotels have a safe for valuables, but it is common for things to go missing from budget hotels. Use your own padlock to lock your baggage or even the room.

Transport terminals are hotspots for theft. There have been several instances of travellers being offered drugged food or drink and then robbed once insensible.

Do not completely trust cab drivers and tourist guides, and make sure to maintain a safe distance. When hiring a car or taxi, ask your hotel to book it for you (or go to a cab rank) and note the licence plate number. Don't wander alone at night especially in deserted parts of the state. Because of Goa's busy nightlife, there are frequent reports of "date rape" or theft due to drugging at trendy bars. If you plan on a night outing make sure you move around in a group.

While visiting places of worship, it's advisable to be respectful of the religious beliefs and dress appropriately. Women should wear clothes that cover the upper arms, and are at least mid-calf length, and take scarves along to cover their heads. Men should avoid shorts and may be asked to cover their heads with a handkerchief or scarf (rather than a hat). It is important for LGBTQ travellers to note that India is a conservative country, so it is best to avoid overt public displays of affection.

Sexual harrassment of women ("eve teasing") is common, especially during festivals. The best response is to point out the perpetrator and exclaim out loud exactly what he has done, as other people will be on your side. Violent attacks on women occasionally occur, so it is advisable to dress conservatively and exercise caution after dark. When queuing for train tickets, use the "ladies' lines", which are usually shorter. On many buses and trains there are "ladies only" seats or compartments. If you need to contact the police, call their **Tourist Helpline** or the **Women's Helpline**; the police also have posts at the airport, main stations, major tourist sights and hotel areas.

Emergency Services

Ambulance, **police** and **fire services** are reliable and can be called from any landline, mobile or phone booth during a crisis.

DIRECTORY

PASSPORTS AND VISAS

Australian High Commission
W india.embassy.gov.au

British High Commission
W ukinindia.fco.gov.uk

Embassy of Canada
W india.gc.ca

Embassy of the United States
W newdelhi.usembassy.gov

Ministry of External Affairs
W mea.gov.in

New Zealand High Commission
W nzembassy.com/india

Visa Office, Australia
W vfsglobal.com/india/australia

Visa Office, Canada
W blsindia-canada.com

Visa Office, UK
W vfsglobal.com/India/UK

Visa Office, USA
W in.ckgs.us

TRAVEL SAFETY ADVICE

Australian Department of Foreign Affairs and Trade
W dfat.gov.au
W smartraveller.gov.au

UK Foreign and Commonwealth Office
W gov.uk/foreign-travel-advice

US Department of State
W travel.state.gov

HEALTH

Apollo Victor Hospital
Station Malbhat, Margao
C 0832 672 8888
W victorhospital.com

Dr Kolwalkar's Galaxy Hospital
Duler, Mapusa
C 0832 226 6666
W galaxyhospital goa.com

Manipal Health Systems Pvt Ltd
Dona Paula, Panaji
C 0832 300 2500
W goa.manipal hospitals.com

Vintage Hospital & Medical Research Centre Pvt Ltd
Santa Inez, Panaji
C 0832 564 4401

Wellness Forever
MG Rd, Panaji
C 0832 242 4884
W wellnessforever.in

PERSONAL SECURITY

Tourist Helpline
C 1 800 111 363

Women's Helpline
C 1091

EMERGENCY SERVICES

Ambulance
C 108

Fire Brigade
C 0832 242 3101

Police
C 100 or 1090

Travellers with Specific Needs

Disabled access has been improving throughout the state to make Goa an enjoyable destination for everyone. The airport is fully accessible to travellers with specific needs, with free transport provided in Kadamba buses as well as in ferries. In 2017 Candolim Beach *(see p12)* became the very first wheelchair accessible beach in India. It also held the first beach festival for people with disabilities, hosting games and activities for them. Boardwalks have been installed at the beach from the starting point right up to the water. There are wheelchairs with special tyres that are easy to steer on sand as well as those that float on water.

Currency and Banking

The local currency is rupees (₹), which come in notes of ₹2,000, ₹500, ₹200, ₹100, ₹50, ₹20, ₹10 and occasionally still ₹5, with coins of ₹10, ₹5, ₹2 and ₹1.

Banks are usually open 10am to mid-afternoon Monday to Friday. Public banks are closed on second and fourth Saturdays of the month. Private bureaux de change are quite common, especially in Panaji and Calangute, and may offer decent rates. Mid- and upper-range hotels exchange foreign currency, but rates are usually poor. ATMs are widespread and accept foreign-issued credit and debit cards

(especially Visa and MasterCard). These two types of credit cards are widely accepted in upmarket shops and restaurants, but they may attract a surcharge.

Telephone and Internet

International and national phone calls can be made easily and relatively cheaply from numerous telephone booths (look for places advertising STD/ISD phone calls). Calls can often be made from hotel rooms, but there may be an exorbitant mark-up, so check rates first. The country code for India is +91; the area code for Goa is 0832.

If you are planning to use your mobile in Goa, check rates and accessibility with your service provider at home. Alternatively, buy a local SIM card (available at phone shops), for an Indian telephone number with access to cheap local phone rates.

Most hotels offer Wi-Fi access, and many bars and cafés provide free Wi-Fi.

Postal Services

There is a handy branch of the **Head Post Office** at Panaji. For poste restante, you will need to go to the **Arambol Post Office**. Packages need to be sealed.

Language

Konkani and English are the official languages of the state of Goa. You will hear Konkani spoken everywhere, but

almost everyone can speak English. Road signs are usually in English as well as in Konkani.

TV, Radio and Newspapers

Most hotel rooms will have a TV offering local and international channels. Local FM radio stations, including **AIR Panaji**, **Gyan Vani**, **Radio Indigo** and **Radio Mirchi**, play Hindi pop; **Big 92.7 FM** plays an international selection.

The English-language newspapers in Goa include *The Times of India* (its local edition has the useful Goa Times supplement) and *Navhind Times*, *O Heraldo* and the *Goa News*. India Today, Zee News, Times Now, NDTV and Republic are among English-language television networks that are broadcasted 24 hours a day.

Opening Hours

Shops typically open from 10am to 6pm Monday to Saturday. Many museums and some tourist sights are closed on Mondays. Popular malls such as **Mall De Goa**, **Caculo Mall** and **Big G** usually open from 10am. Shops and markets remain closed on national holidays.

Time Difference

Goa is on Indian Standard Time (IST), which is 5.5 hours ahead of Greenwich Mean Time (GMT), 9.5 hours ahead of New York, 12.5 hours ahead of Los Angeles, and 4.5 hours behind Sydney.

Electrical Appliances

The electricity supply is 220V AC. Most sockets are triple round-pin but take European-size double round-pin plugs. British, Irish and Australasian devices will only need an adaptor, while North American devices will need an adaptor and a converter.

Driving and Traffic Rules

Carry an international driving licence if you plan on driving yourself. You also need to be well prepared for the traffic rules and road conditions in Goa. In India, driving is on the left and vehicles give way to the right. While driving on the highway, be careful of large vehicles, which often use muscle power to force you off the road. It is mandatory to wear a helmet if you are riding a two-wheeler, else you may be stopped by the police and fined. Speed limits range from 30 kmph (19 mph) to 60 kmph (37 mph). Drive slowly and look out for speed breakers especially at night, as the streets are poorly lit. The blood alcohol limit for drivers is 0.03% – which is equal to one drink.

Weather

The best time to visit Goa is during winter (November–March). Goa can be extremely hot and humid from April to May (reaching 30°C/86°F), and rather wet from June until September, when the monsoon kicks in. The weather from November to March stays warm and sunny, with cool evenings. April to October are the months between peak and off-peak seasons when the beaches are quieter. Keep in mind that most of the restaurants might be closed during off season, and the seas are too rough for swimming or venturing out in boats.

Cruises

Goa offers various types of cruises on both the Mandovi River, as well as the Arabian Sea. There are floating restaurants and casino cruises as well. Two notable cruises are **Angriya** and **Galaxy Galante**. Angriya is India's first domestic luxury cruise liner that sails between Mumbai and Goa on the Arabian Sea. It is complete with all amenities that include accommodation, dining and entertainment. The Galaxy Galante sails on the Mandovi River. It is a floating restaurant and a nightclub as well. Cruises on the Mandovi offer lovely views of the city and its old buildings, and also gain access to the back-waters of Goa, passing through the Chorão and Divar Islands.

DIRECTORY

POSTAL SERVICES

Arambol Post Office
MAP G2 ▪ 274/1, MDR17, Arambol ▪ Open 9:30am–3pm Mon–Sat

Head Post Office
MAP K6 ▪ Mahatma Gandhi Rd, Patto Colony, Panaji ▪ Open 9:30am–3:30pm Mon–Sat

TV, RADIO AND NEWSPAPERS

AIR Panaji
105.4 MHz
ⓦ irpanaji.gov.in

Big 92.7 FM
92.7 MHz
ⓦ 927bigfm.com

Gyan Vani
107.8 MHz

Radio Indigo
91.9 MHz

Radio Mirchi
98.3 MHz
ⓦ radiomirchi.com

Goa News
ⓦ goanews.com

Navhind Times
ⓦ navhindtimes.in

O Heraldo
ⓦ heraldgoa.in

The Times of India
ⓦ timesofindia.
indiatimes.com/goa

OPENING HOURS

Big G
MAP K6 ▪ Dr Dada Vaidya Rd, Altinho, Panaji
ⓒ (0832) 243 4723

Caculo Mall
MAP K6 ▪ 16 Shanta, St Inez Rd, Panaji
ⓒ (0832) 223 3300

Mall De Goa
MAP K5 ▪ NH17, Alto Porvorim, Penha de Franca

CRUISES

Angriya
ⓦ angriyacruises.com

Galaxy Galante
ⓦ galaxiagalante.in

Visitor Information

Tourist offices provide advice on sightseeing and detailed maps of the city, which can also be found in most bookshops. The **Goa Tourism Development Corporation (GTDC)** website has information and itineraries. Check for packages and events well in advance of your arrival. They also provide hotel bookings.

Trips and Tours

Walking and cycling tours are popular among visitors coming to Goa. A walking tour around the city is best described as a walk through time, which includes historical details and local trivia given by a tour guide. There are full-day tours of North and South Goa, the Dudhsagar Falls and Spice Plantations, as well as a chance to explore the hidden trails at Udaan Dongor. Several exciting packages are offered by **Thrillophilia**.

Cycling tours are best to witness the natural beauty of the state. Tour packages are available online for cycling through Old Goa as well as Chorão and Divar Islands. Snacks and drinks are provided. Make sure that you wear comfortable footwear. Check the websites of **Kalypso Adventures**, **Wandertrails**, **Adventure Breaks** and **Adventure Nation** for various cycling tours. E-bike tours are also becoming incredibly popular, with the concept of smooth and effortless riding while exploring the city. **B:live** offers a myriad of e-bike tours.

Swimming and Watersports

Due to the tropical weather Goa's seas have a pleasant temperature to swim in. Areas that are safe for swimming have been marked with red and yellow flags and life guards monitor beaches during strong currents and rip tides. During monsoons, stay away from the sea due to high tides. It is wise to swim during the day, and October to May is the best time.

Watersports ranging from windsurfing to jet skiing, are offered at the beaches. Enjoy kayaking at sunset, or adventure sports such as white-water rafting and sea-rafting. **Flying Fish** offers snorkelling and scuba diving at Grande Island.

Shopping

A wide array of crafts from all over India are available in Goa. Markets such as **Mapusa Market**, **Arpora's Saturday Night Bazaar** and **Anjuna Flea Market** (see pp62–3) offer local handicrafts, spices, pickles and textiles at negotiable prices.

Shops sell textiles by the metre, so buy some fabric and have your clothes tailored at affordable prices. **Sacha's Shop** (see p78), **Hollywood Fashion** and **Jade Jagger** are popular boutiques that stitch customized garments.

Stores such as **Aparant Goan Handicrafts Emporium** (see p78) sell local handicrafts. **Shalala Handicrafts** is another notable store offering handmade carpets in silk and wool as well as unique jewellery.

It's worth checking prices and quality before heading elsewhere. Bargaining is de rigueur in bazaars and most small shops, but not usually in malls and government emporiums. Top buys include cashew nuts, wines and spices, found easily in Panaji. You can also find bookstores here.

Casinos and Gambling

Goa is one of the few states in India where casino gambling has been legalized. It is popular for the casino cruises that sail on the Mandovi River. Make sure you are aware of the gambling rules in casinos.

All visitors are obligated by law to pay an entry fee of ₹700 in order to receive a receipt for government levy. Keep this slip handy at all times. To be found inside a casino without this slip is a punishable offence. Smoking is prohibited, although some places have VIP smoking rooms. Contact the casino and inquire in advance.

Only visitors who are older than 21 years of age are allowed to enter the gaming areas at the casinos. It is illegal for under 21s to gamble, but other areas such as restaurants, might be open for all.

Goa's casinos host two types of gambling games – Slot Games and Table Games. Slot machines are not as popular as the table games, since they do not have a high pay out. Most machines accept cash, and pay outs need to be collected from the attendants. Table games include – baccarat, money wheel, blackjack, Texas hold'em poker, roulette and many more. For roulette the minimum bet starts at ₹50, while for other games it is ₹100. A variety of gaming chips are used, but cash chips, OTP chips and rolling chips are commonly used.

Casinos have stringent dress codes. Wear semi-formal attire and avoid shorts or flip-flops. To improve your chances of success, take breaks rather than gambling non-stop, as fatigue can cloud your judgement. Don't spend more than an hour deciding whether to "hold' em" or "fold 'em", or spend too much time over a slot machine, you could experience fatigue.

In case you get lucky and win, be tactful about how you react. Do not boast about your winnings as strangers might hear you.

Dining

Goan cuisine is a fusion of the various cultures that it has encountered over the centuries. Vegetarian food is available in some places, but it is not a speciality of the state. Traditional dishes are usually rich in coconut milk, cashews and local spices, such as tamarind, kokum and red Goan chillies. Meats such as pork and beef are favourites among the locals, and seafood is a speciality. The staple food here is fish curry and rice. You can find tuna, kingfish, shark, mackerel and pomfret. Prawns, crabs and lobsters are also crowd pleasers.

Restaurants are mostly child-friendly, and if children find spicy food hard to deal with, there are many alternatives including cafés, Chinese eateries, international chains and multi-cuisine restaurants among others. The fast-food chains have altered their menus to suit the local palate. Eateries from luxurious gourmet restaurants as well as small cafés and roadside stalls, offer a mix of intercontinental cuisine.

Accommodation

Goa has a wide range of accommodation options, from five-star hotels to mid-range budget and even backpacker lodges. You are likely to find a room to suit your budget wherever you go, but it is best to make reservations in advance. Rates for midrange accommodation are a bargain by Western standards. **Airbnb** is very useful for locating places to stay. **Couchsurfing**, which allows travellers to book to stay with a family for a short period, is also available in Goa. You could also book a room via the **OYO Rooms** mobile app as it offers good discounts.

Keep in mind that prices are likely to be higher during peak season, especially during Christmas and New Year. The months between April to October are considered off-peak. This is when you can find discounted hotel rates. Travellers should also be aware that the government of India has imposed luxury taxes on hotels.

DIRECTORY

VISITOR INFORMATION

GTDC
2nd Floor, Paryatan Bhavan, Panaji
0832 243 7132
goa-tourism.com

TRIPS AND TOURS

Adventure Breaks
adventurebreaks.in

Adventure Nation
0124 4983580
adventurenation.com

B:live
blive.co.in

Kalypso Adventures
2336 3607
kalypsoadventures.com

Thrillophilia
thrillophilia.com

Wandertrails
wandertrails.com

SWIMMING AND WATERSPORTS

Flying Fish
flyingfish.in

SHOPPING

Hollywood Fashion
Fort Aguada Rd, Candolim
099 6019 2580

Jade Jagger
Ashvem Beach
0897 506 1040
jadejagger.co.uk

Shalala Handicrafts
Shalala Residency, Calangute
0832 652 8672
shalalahandicrafts.info

ACCOMMODATION

Airbnb
airbnb.com

Couchsurfing
couchsurfing.com

OYO Rooms
oyorooms.com

Places to Stay

PRICE CATEGORIES
For a standard, double room per night (with breakfast if included), taxes and extra charges.

₹ under ₹3,000   ₹₹ ₹3,000–7,000   ₹₹₹ over ₹7,000

Luxury Hotels

Alila Diwa
MAP A5 ■ 48/10, Adao Waddo, Majorda ■ 0832 274 6800 ■ www.alila hotels.com ■ ₹₹₹
Architecturally inspiring, this resort, close to Majorda Beach, overlooks the Arabian Sea. There are 153 spacious guestrooms and suites and four great restaurants. Everything is state-of-the-art, down to the wood-lined loft rooms and 40 inch large plasma TVs. Indulge in Ayurvedic or Balinese spa treatments or lounge by the sea-facing infinity pool.

Caravela Beach Resort
MAP L2 ■ Varca Beach, Fatrade, Margao ■ 0832 669 5000 ■ www.caravela beachresortgoa.com ■ ₹₹₹
Set amid vast lawns, the classical Portuguese-style architecture of this resort blends its traditional charm with contemporary luxuries. Facilities include beach access, an outdoor pool, a golf course, and a variety of restaurants.

Cidade de Goa
MAP K6 ■ Opp. Manipal Hospitals, Vainguinim Beach, Panaji ■ 0832 245 4545 ■ www.cidadede goa.com ■ ₹₹₹
Designed by architect Charles Correa, the Cidade de Goa or "City of Goa" has luxurious rooms and suites, some with stunning sea views. It houses five restaurants, two sleek bars and a casino on site. The resort also offers an array of watersports and organized activities.

Goa Marriott Resort & Spa
MAP J6 ■ Miramar, Panaji ■ 0832 246 3333 ■ www. marriott.com ■ ₹₹₹
Offering sweeping views of the Arabian Sea, this resort is located in the heart of the city. Facilities include stylish restaurants, a swimming pool as well as a spa and fitness centre.

Holiday Inn Resort Goa
MAP L2 ■ Mobor Beach, Cavelossim ■ 0832 287 0000 ■ www.ihg.com ■ ₹₹₹
With direct access to the Mobor Beach, this resort blends traditional Goan architecture with contemporary styles. It is equipped with an activity zone for kids, an outdoor pool and a spa offering multiple Ayurvedic treatments. It houses several restaurants, as well as a bar that has sunset views.

Kenilworth Beach Resort & Spa
MAP L2 ■ Majorda-Utorda Rd ■ 0832 669 8888 ■ www.kenilworth hotels.com ■ ₹₹₹
Situated in Salcete, this luxury hotel is a walk away from the beach. Its rooms are spacious and facilities are state-of-the-art. Enjoy a dip in the pool, or relax at the on-site spa facility. With the beach close by, visitors can indulge in seasonal watersports.

The LaLiT Golf & Spa Resort Goa
MAP D6 ■ Raj Baga, Canacona ■ 0832 266 7777 ■ www.thelalit.com ■ ₹₹₹
A gorgeous lobby flanked by two grand staircases greets visitors at this hotel. Rooms are stylish with some overlooking the landscaped gardens and the nine-hole golf course. Watersport activities, sunset cruises, yoga and fishing are on offer.

The Leela Goa
MAP D5 ■ Mobor, Cavelossim ■ 0832 662 1234 ■ www.theleela. com ■ ₹₹₹
A landmark in Cavelossim, the Leela Goa has a secluded beach, fresh-water lagoons and is known for its impeccable hospitality. The hotel boasts an award-winning spa, a golf course and a children's activity centre.

Radisson Blu Resort
MAP L2 ■ Cavelossim Beach, Mobor Beach ■ 0832 672 6666 ■ www. radissonblu.com ■ ₹₹₹
A ten-minute walk from the Arabian Sea, this Portuguese-style resort is lush with gardens and has direct access to the beach. On site are two swimming pools, a spa, three restaurants and a bar.

Taj Exotica Resort & Spa

MAP A6 ▪ Calwaddo, Salcete, Benaulim ▪ 0832 668 3333 ▪ www.taj hotels.com ▪ ₹₹₹

Set amid tropical gardens, the Taj Exotica exudes quiet elegance and luxury. Goan- and Portuguese-style rooms, with sea or garden views, have private verandas. The beachfront Lobster Shack offers excellent seafood, while Allegria is known for its authentic Goan cuisine.

Taj Fort Aguada Resort & Spa

MAP H5 ▪ Sinquerim, Candolim ▪ 0832 664 5858 ▪ www.tajhotels. com ▪ ₹₹₹

Built on the ramparts of the 17th-century Fort Aguada, this hotel is the epitome of old-world style. It has 145 rooms, villas and cottages, some with great sea views. There are also exclusive villas and cottages on a hillside behind the resort.

Taj Vivanta

MAP L2 ▪ St Anne's Junction, Dayanand Bandodkar Marg, Panaji ▪ 0832 663 3636 ▪ www. tajhotels.com ▪ ₹₹₹

This Taj property is located In the heart of Panjim. With its fresh look and ambience, it appeals to the international traveller. The contemporary-style rooms are charming.

W Goa

MAP H4 ▪ Vagator Beach ▪ 0832 671 8888 ▪ www. starwoodhotels.com ▪ ₹₹₹

Tucked on a hillside above Vagator, W's flamboyant lobby leads to the Woo Bar, which has its own DJ console. The rooms are just as impressive, and come in categories, such as Wonderful, Fabulous and Spectacular. The Kitchen Table is an all-day diner, while the Spice Traders serves pan-Asian cuisine. There's also a Clarins spa on site.

Boutique and Heritage Hotels

Cavala Resort

MAP L2 ▪ Calangute-Baga Rd, Calangute ▪ 0839 005 5518 ▪ ₹₹

Dating back to 1979, the ivy-clad structure of Cavala immediately stands out. Goan architect Lucio Miranda designed this two-storeyed hotel with exposed laterite, tiled roof and *balcãos* (balconies) making it truly a vintage Goa property. The popular on-site bar is always crowded.

Coconut Creek Resort

MAP L2 ▪ Bimmut Ward, Bogmalo ▪ 0832 253 8090 ▪ www.coconut creekgoa.com ▪ ₹₹

Located on Bogmalo Beach, this tranquil resort is surrounded by lush palms and a meandering creek. It offers luxurious rooms with views of landscaped gardens. Facilities include a swimming pool, spa and a salon.

Estrela Do Mar Beach Resort

MAP L2 ▪ Opp. Our Lady of Piety Chapel, Calangute-Baga Rd ▪ 0805 550 1234 ▪ ₹₹

Close to Calangute Beach, this resort provides great views of the sea from its Swiss cottage-style rooms. It is popular with adventure seekers and music enthusiasts as it is set near all the nightlife hubs and bazaars.

Heritage Village Resort & Spa

MAP L2 ▪ Arossim Beach Rd, Cansaulim, Arossim ▪ 0832 669 4444 ▪ www. selecthotels.co.in ▪ ₹₹

This pet-friendly resort is located near Arossim and Cansaulim Beach. It is lush with landscaped gardens, and boasts a swimming pool with a separate kid's section. Enjoy the Turkish bath facilities as well as the yoga offered here.

Lemon Tree Hotel Candolim

MAP L2 ▪ Pinto Waddo, Candolim ▪ 0832 248 9750 ▪ www.lemontree hotels.com ▪ ₹₹

Close to the Anjuna and Candolim beaches, this hotel is 5 km (3 miles) away from the 17th-century Fort Aguada. The rooms have contemporary designs, with balconies and access to a private pool. There is a vibrant café, terrace-top bar as well as a fitness centre on site.

Mateus

MAP K6 ▪ 432 Rua 31 de Janeiro, Fontainhas, Panaji ▪ 0744 748 8889 ▪ www.mateusgoa.com ▪ ₹₹

Set in a restored 1879 Portuguese mansion, this boutique hotel is conveniently located, close to the restaurants and waterfront in Fontainhas. It offers nine tastefully decorated rooms and has good service. Bike and car rentals are available.

Montego Bay Beach Village
MAP L2 ▪ Vithaldas Waddo, Morjim ▪ 0982 215 0847 ▪ www.montego baygoa.com ▪ ₹₹
Shaded with coconut groves, this hotel offers accommodation in beach huts that have air-conditioning. They have an outdoor pool and a restaurant. Enjoy yoga lessons or go for a dolphin-spotting trip.

Panjim Inn & Panjim Pousada
MAP K6 ▪ E-212, 31st January Rd, Fontainhas, Panaji ▪ 0832 222 6523 ▪ www.panjiminn.com ▪ ₹₹
A 300-year-old townhouse, now a heritage hotel, with period furniture. The adjacent three-storeyed wing overlooks the Mandovi, while the Pousada annexe across the road has two lovely rooms sharing a wooden balcony that overlooks a courtyard.

Rio Boutique
MAP L2 ▪ Ambekhand, Reis Magos, Bardez-Goa ▪ 0832 249 1950 ▪ www.rioboutiquegoa.com ▪ ₹₹
Walking distance from Reis Magos Fort and Coco Beach, this hotel stands out with its sleek design, professional service and friendly staff. Each room is characterized with Resort Rio's signature style. Facilities include Moroccon-inspired decor, a pool, Ayurvedic spa centre and a restaurant.

Taj Holiday Village Resort and Spa
MAP L2 ▪ Sinquerim, Candolim ▪ 0832 664 5858 ▪ www.tajhotels.com ▪ ₹₹
This elegant property offers 39 luxurious rooms

and suites. The stunning rooftop infinity pool offers bird's eye views of the surroundings and an unparalleled bathing experience. The night-club, SinQ, makes it a popular choice.

Tree House Sonnet
MAP L2 ▪ Panchayat Rd, Anjuna ▪ 0913 006 2454, 0913 006 2452 ▪ www.treehousehotels.in ▪ ₹₹
A popular property with well-equipped rooms and cheerful service, this hotel is value for money. It is walking distance from the Anjuna Flea Market and Vagator Beach. Facilities include an indoor swimming pool and a sun terrace. Free Wi-Fi.

Vivenda Dos Palhacos
MAP A5 ▪ Costa Vaddo, Majorda ▪ 0832 322 1119 ▪ www.vivendagoa.com ▪ ₹₹
A mix of Indo-Portuguese elegance and boutique chic, this heritage guesthouse occupies a 100-year-old *palacio*. Beautifully furnished by owners Simon and Charlotte Hayward, the seven inviting rooms have four-poster beds and colonial furniture. Interestingly, the rooms are named after places where the family has stayed. Guests can enjoy a drink at the Lorry Back Bar *(see p102)*, which is actually a converted lorry.

Aashyana Lakhanpal
MAP H5 ▪ Escrivao Vaddo, Candolim ▪ 0832 248 9276 ▪ www.aashyana lakhanpal.com ▪ ₹₹₹
Chic Aashyana Lakhanpal, close to Candolim Beach, has a stylish five-bedroom villa, three secluded

casinhas (little houses) and two Portuguese-style bungalows, all tastefully furnished. There's also a fabulous diamond-shaped pool and Ayurvedic spa.

Acron Waterfront Resort
MAP L2 ▪ Seaward side of Baga Bridge, Baga ▪ 0772 201 6888 ▪ www.acron waterfrontresortgoa.com ▪ ₹₹₹
A part of the ITC Fortune Hotel in Goa, this resort extends across the Baga peninsula. The rooms provide modern amenities in a rustic setting. In close proximity to the beach and the market, it is a popular choice. There is a spa and wellness centre on site.

Ahilya by the Sea
MAP J6 ▪ 787 Nerul-Reis Margos Rd, Nerul ▪ 0845 938 6478 ▪ www.ahilya bythesea.com ▪ ₹₹₹
Overlooking Coco Beach, Ahilya by the Sea features charming Balinese-style villas, which have seven cosy rooms. The many highlights of staying here include the superb infinity pool and a treehouse spa, which offers massages.

Casa Palacio Siolim House
MAP J3 ▪ 62/1, opp. Wadi Chapel, Siolim ▪ 0982 258 4560 ▪ www.siolimhouse.com ▪ ₹₹₹
An elegantly converted 350-year-old villa, which was once the residence of the governor of Macao. Antique-furnished rooms and suites are ranged around a pillared courtyard. Some have no air conditioning or TV. Guests can also stay next door at the pretty, Little Siolim.

Casa Vagator

MAP H4 ▪ H. No. 594/4, Vozran, Vagator ▪ 0703 091 3923 ▪ www.casa boutiquehotels.com ▪ ₹₹₹
Smart and stylish Casa Vagator offers deluxe doubles and luxury options, furnished with sofas. Artworks and handpicked artifacts feature in all the rooms. The terrace bar is a great place to enjoy sunset views. Next door is the noisy Nine Bar, which plays trance beats from 4pm to midnight.

Elsewhere

For booking, email: gaze @aseascape.com ▪ www. aseascape.com ▪ ₹₹₹
Goa's best kept secret, the location of this beachfront property is only revealed if you are a registered guest. A collection of dreamy 19th-century villas, named the Piggery, Bakery, Priest's House and Captain's House, are separated from the mainland by a saltwater creek and can only be accessed via a bamboo footbridge. There are three creek-facing luxury tents too. A minimum one-week stay is required. Elsewhere remains closed from June to September.

Fort Tiracol Heritage Hotel

MAP G1 ▪ Pernem Taluka, Tiracol ▪ 0772 005 6799 ▪ www.forttiracol.in ▪ ₹₹₹
The seven luxurious rooms here are decorated in traditional Lusitanian ochre and white, with oxide floors, wrought-iron furniture and Indian textiles. The rooms have private balconies with sea views. The restaurant and lounge-bar (see p71) on the first floor offers authentic Goan food.

Nilaya Hermitage

MAP H4 ▪ Arpora, Bhati Bardez ▪ 0832 227 6793 ▪ www.nilaya.com ▪ ₹₹₹
Set on a hilltop retreat away from the bustling beaches, Nilaya (or hidden dwelling) offers matchless views over the coastal plain. The rooms are beautiful and open onto a tiled pool. A dhow (teak sailing vessel) takes guests on cruises up the river.

Pousada Tauma

MAP H5 ▪ Porba Vaddo, Calangute ▪ 0976 580 4964 ▪ www.pousada-tauma.com ▪ ₹₹₹
This small, luxury resort has double-storey laterite villas ranged around a pool. Each has its own private dining area and patio, with a garden or terrace. The open-air Copper Bowl restaurant serves Goan food. A range of Ayurvedic treatments are available.

Rockheart Goa

MAP H5 ▪ 14 A/10 Annavaddo, Candolim ▪ 0981 932 7284 ▪ www. rockheartgoa.com ▪ ₹₹₹
At Rockheart Goa, guests can enjoy the luxury villa experience created by legendary author Frank Simoes and his wife Gita. Close to Candolim Beach, this place has two lovely bedrooms and one guest cottage, all equipped with modern facilities.

Mid-Range Hotels

A's Holiday Beach Resort

MAP A5 ▪ Sunset Beach, Betalbatim ▪ 0982 238 1029 ▪ www.aholiday resort.com ▪ ₹₹
Stay at duplex villas, with private balconies that overlook the garden and beach. There is an outdoor swimming pool and a massage parlour too.

Cavala Resort

MAP H5 ▪ Calangute-Baga Rd, Calangute ▪ 0832 227 7587 ▪ www. cavala.com ▪ ₹₹
A great seaside location, intimate ambience, an excellent restaurant and bar are among the few reasons to stay at Cavala. The comfortable single, double and twin-bedded rooms are quiet despite the roadside location. All open onto a balcony, or sit-out area.

Granpa's Inn Hotel Bougainvillea

MAP H4 ▪ Gaunwadi, Anjuna–Mausa Rd, Anjuna ▪ 0866 965 6396 ▪ www.granpasinn.com ▪ ₹₹
Set amid lush gardens with a pool and terrace, is a 200-year-old Portuguese-styled mansion. There are three categories of rooms and suites; ancestral suites and standard rooms at the main house; and the poolside suites, with verandas and kitchenettes.

Island House Goa

MAP L5 ▪ No. 45, Piedade, Goltim, Divar ▪ 0832 228 0605 ▪ www.islandhouse goa.com ▪ ₹₹
A lovely Indo-Portuguese house with comfortable rooms, a bar, meditation area, pool and duck pond. From bird-watching to fishing, there are plenty of activities for guests here. Goan dishes and international fare is served in the dining area, which overlooks the pool and garden.

For a key to hotel price categories see p114

La Cabana Beach & Spa

MAP G3 ▪ Ashvem Beach, Ashvem Wada, Mandrem ▪ 0982 283 5550 ▪ www.lacabana.in ▪ ₹₹

Stay in either the luxury tents, cosy cottages or villas at La Cabana. The air-conditioned tents have flat-screen TVs, minibars and sit-out areas. Some villas have sea views. Amenities include an outdoor pool and a beachfront restaurant. The spa offers treatments and therapies.

La Maison Fontainhas

MAP L2 ▪ 5/158, near St Sebastian Chapel Fontainhas, Panaji ▪ 0832 223 5555 ▪ ₹₹

Located in the atmospheric Latin Quarter, this cosy family-run heritage home boasts beautiful and elegant interiors. Beautiful artworks line the walls of the simple yet chic rooms with en-suite bathrooms. The European Fusion restaurant, Desbue, offers a creative menu.

La Vie Woods

MAP H5 ▪ Calangute-Baga Rd, next to Mirabai Restaurant, Calangute ▪ 0832 651 1944 ▪ www.laviewoods.com ▪ ₹₹

A perfect place for couples and families, La Vie Woods is within walking distance of Calangute Beach. It features 22 two-storey Swiss-style chalets, which overlook the outdoor pool. All cottages are air conditioned and have LCD TVs.

The Mandala

MAP H2 ▪ Mandrem-Ashvem Rd, Mandrem ▪ 0981 150 0069 ▪ www.themandalagoa.space ▪ ₹₹

Painted murals adorn the walls of this eco-resort. Opt to stay in bamboo huts or at the rooms in the Art House, with views of the lake. There are two-tier nomadic villas too model-led as Kerala houseboats. Daily yoga classes are available and an organic restaurant is on site.

Nanutel

MAP B5 ▪ Padre Miranda Rd, opp. to Club Harmonia, Margao ▪ 0832 672 2222 ▪ www.nanuhotels.in ▪ ₹₹

Centrally located, this three-star hotel is ideal for business travellers. Margao's bus and rail-way station are 2 km (1.2 miles) away. There are 55 well-appointed rooms and a multi-cuisine restaurant next to the pool. A travel desk helps guests plan their sightseeing itinerary.

Riva Beach Resort

MAP G2 ▪ Mandrem Beach Rd, Pernem ▪ 0832 224 7612 ▪ www.rivaresorts.com ▪ ₹₹

A casual riverfront resort, Riva has eco-friendly riverfront cottages and spacious suites with sea views. The multi-cuisine Buddha Grill restaurant has a coffee shop next door. Ayurvedic treatments are available at the spa.

Soul Vacation

MAP A5 ▪ 4th Ward, Colva Beach, Colva ▪ 0832 278 8186 ▪ www.soulvacation.in ▪ ₹₹

A short stroll away from Colva Beach, this concept spa resort has comfortable rooms with Mediterranean design, which open out onto the pool. The spa has an in-house Ayurvedic specialist and the café has indoor and oudoor seating. Free Wi-Fi is available in public areas only.

Budget Hotels

Alba Rooms Palolem

MAP L2 ▪ Palolem Beach Rd, Palolem, Canacona ▪ 0992 356 9948 ▪ www.albaroomspalolem.com ▪ ₹

Just 30 m (33 yards) away from the beach's main entrance, you will find a green way to the lovely garden of this hotel. The rooms are clean and well-lit, fully-equipped with modern amenities. The personalized attention from owner, Sanjay, makes the stay great.

The Banyan Soul

MAP H4 ▪ No. 962(1), off Flea Market Rd, Anjuna ▪ 0982 070 7283 ▪ www.thebanyansoul.com ▪ ₹

On the quiet southeastern fringes of Anjuna, this chic designer hotel has attractively deco-rated rooms, each with a private outdoor sitting area. Guests can relax in the lounge area under an old banyan tree. There's an outdoor library here too.

Hotel Mayfair

MAP K6 ▪ Dr Dada Vaidya Rd, near Mahalaxmi Temple, Panaji ▪ 0832 222 3317 ▪ www.erahotels.com/hotel-mayfair/ ▪ ₹

In the heart of Panaji, Mayfair features charming

decor inspired by famous cartoonist Mario Miranda's works. The tastefully decorated air-conditioned rooms have modern amenities.

Martin's Comfort

MAP L2 ▪ Ranwaddo, Betalbatim ▪ 0832 288 0765 ▪ www.martins comfort.com ▪ ₹

Situated in the village of Betalbatim, this resort is managed and owned by the same people who run the popular eatery by the same name, situated a few blocks away. With its Goan architecture and antique Portuguese-style furniture, this place gives its visitors a glimpse of Goan history.

Neptune Point Beach Resort

MAP L2 ▪ Opp. Dental clinic, Palolem, Canacona ▪ 0915 843 2629 ▪ www. huts-palolem.com ▪ ₹

Some rooms at this resort overlook the beach. The en-suite rooms are equipped with basic amenities, comfortable mattresses and air-conditioning. It also organizes the famed headphone parties in Palolem.

Oceanic

MAP D6 ▪ Palolem-Patnem Beach Rd, Tembewado, Canacona ▪ 0832 264 3059 ▪ www. oceanicgoa.com ▪ ₹

About a 10-minute walk inland from Palolem Beach, Oceanic's stylishly designed marble-floored rooms are fresh and relaxing. There is a pool on a forested patio as well as an excellent restaurant and bar.

Old Goa Residency

MAP M6 ▪ Near Fire Brigade, Velha Goa ▪ 0832 228 5327 ▪ ₹

Run by the Goa Tourism Development Corporation (GTDC), this hotel has modern rooms with basic amenities. Set in Old Goa, it is located close to the beautiful churches in the area. No Wi-Fi.

Ruffles Beach Resort

MAP H5 ▪ Fort Aguada Rd, Vaddi Beach, opp. State Bank of India, Candolim ▪ 0838 007 2662 ▪ www.rufflesgoa. com ▪ ₹

Close to Candolim Beach, this resort has well-equipped modern rooms and a courtyard pool. There are two multi-cuisine restaurants as well as a poolside bar.

Hotel Sun Inn

MAP D3 ▪ Opp. Maruti Temple, Varkhandem, Ponda ▪ 0832 231 8180 ▪ www.hotelsuninn.com ▪ ₹₹

A multi-storey business hotel, Hotel Sun Inn is a short distance away from Central Ponda. Choose from a range of deluxe, executive twin and pre-mium interconnected rooms here. An in-house restaurant serves good traditional Indian food.

Palm Grove Cottages

MAP A6 ▪ House No. 1678, Tamdi Mati, Benaulim ▪ 0832 277 0059 ▪ www. palm grovegoa.com ▪ ₹₹

Surrounded by pretty gardens, secluded Palm Grove is a 15-minute walk away from Benaulim Beach. All rooms have en-suite bathrooms, while some have private balconies. The deluxe rooms are in a separate Portuguese-style annexe. On site is an alfresco garden restaurant that serves excellent sea-food dishes. Some rooms have Wi-Fi.

B&Bs and Guesthouses

Heaven Goa

MAP A6 ▪ H. No. 104/3, Pedda, Sernabatim ▪ 0832 277 2201 ▪ www. heavengoa.in ▪ ₹

This welcoming Swiss-run guesthouse has a dozen clean rooms, well set up with double beds, en-suite bathrooms and balconies.

Indian Kitchen

MAP H5 ▪ 6/3A, Calangute–Baga Rd, Shiroli Pulachi, Calangute ▪ 0832 227 7555 ▪ www. indiankitchen-goa.com ▪ ₹

Brightly patterned walls featuring mosaic tiling adorn the rooms of this guesthouse. Rooms range from basic to spacious apartments and wooden chalets, and are equipped with a fridge, a TV and a sit-out area. There is an extra charge for air-conditioned rooms and Wi-Fi. A pool and an Indian restaurant are on site.

Hospedaria Abrido de Botelho

MAP L2 ▪ Rua De Natal, Fontainhas, Panaji ▪ 0952 777 8884 ▪ www. hadbgoa.com ▪ ₹₹

This heritage hotel has large, tastefully decorated rooms with beautiful wooden and tiled floors. Breakfast is served in the rear garden.

Kate's Cottages
MAP D6 ■ Behind Hi-Tide Coco Huts, Palolem Beach, Canacona ■ 0904 924 0014 ■ www.kates cottagesgoa.com ■ ₹₹
South of Palolem Beach is a wooden cottage. The two air-conditioned rooms, on the first floor above Fern's restaurant, are en-suite rooms with four-poster beds and sea views. Both rooms have independent entrances. There are also rooms on the ground floor.

Lotus Sutra
MAP G2 ■ Khalcha Wada, Arambol Beach, Arambol ■ 0914 609 6940 ■ www. lotussutragoa.com ■ ₹₹
Some of these deluxe air-conditioned wooden cottages, have sea views, and others offer garden views. Rooms with modern amenities and balconies are available. The restaurant and bar has live music.

Michele's Garden Guesthouse & Café
MAP H4 ■ H. No 955, La Vie En Rose, Anjuna ■ 0832 645 2601 ■ www. michelesgarden.business. site ■ ₹₹
In the heart of Anjuna, this guesthouse has four simple rooms, with en-suite bathrooms and balconies. The garden café, La Vie En Rose is open for breakfast only.

Beach Shacks

Chattai Beach Huts
MAP D6 ■ Ourem, 81/5 Palolem Beach, Canacona ■ 0877 964 8553 ■ www. chattai.co.in ■ ₹
One of Palolem's more stylish options, comprising six well-spaced huts made of *chattai* (straw mats)

right on the beach. All have double beds and attached bathrooms with sit-out areas. Quality mattresses and mosquito nets are provided. Wi-Fi is available in the restaurant area only. Book in advance.

Dunes Holiday Village
MAP G2 ■ Junas Waddo, Mandrem ■ 0832 224 7219 ■ www.dunesgoa.com ■ ₹
The traditional bamboo beach huts or tree houses at Dunes have twin beds and en-suite rooms equipped with safety lockers. A multi-cuisine restaurant offers buffet and à la carte meals. Free Wi-Fi.

Agonda White Sand
MAP D5 ■ Near the Cross, Dhawalkhazan, Agonda, Canacona ■ www.agonda whitesand.com ■ ₹₹
Made of local wood, thatch and bamboo, with stone-tiled floors, the cottages are well furnished and ranged around a busy resto-bar. The luxurious beach villas are Balinese style boutique chalets, with lovely sea views from the private terraces. Minimum three nights stay.

Anahata Retreat
MAP G3 ■ Ashvem Beach, Mandrem ■ 0982 259 0123 ■ www.anahata retreat.com ■ ₹₹
Just north of La Plage restaurant, this retreat has 11 octagonal huts made from dark mango wood. Some are located in the garden, others on the beach and a few have sea views. The well-spaced huts have verandas with good ventilation and quality beds. There is a yoga space and a good restaurant as well as a lounge area on the beach.

Ciaran's Camp
MAP D6 ■ House No. 233/A, Palolem Beach ■ 0832 264 3477 ■ www. ciarans.com ■ ₹₹
A short distance away from the beach, Ciaran's features luxurious coir and coconut-wood huts. Each has mosquito nets, hammocks and bathrooms. Some have roof-level sundecks, daybeds to laze on and to enjoy sea views. On site is a multi-cuisine restaurant and a spa centre.

Little Palm Grove
MAP G3 ■ Ashvem Beach ■ 0965 706 3046 ■ www. palmgrovebeachresort. com ■ ₹₹
On Ashvem Beach, this chic place has six bamboo huts, built from sustainable materials. Some offer sea views. The well-ventilated huts feature en-suite rooms with comfortable beds, as well as a sit-out area.

Yab Yum Resort
MAP G3 ■ Ashvem Beach, Mandrem ■ 0866 969 2229 ■ www.yabyum resorts.com ■ ₹₹
Hidden amid palm groves, this property's distinctive dome-shaped huts are made from palm thatch, mango wood and laterite. There are en-suite rooms but no air conditioning. They feature five Goan cottages too. Yoga and babysitting facilities are available.

Dwarka Eco Beach Resort
MAP D5 ■ Cola Beach Rd, Mattimol, Canacona, Cola ■ 0982 337 7025 ■ www. dwarkagoa.com ■ ₹₹₹
An idyllic beach resort with ten paddy-thatch cabins on the edge of a freshwater lagoon, which can be crossed via a footbridge. The

simply furnished huts with private bathrooms feature a seating area, some have balconies. There is an outdoor swimming pool and bar. Free Wi-Fi is available.

Leela Cottages
MAP G3 ■ Morjim-Mandrem Rd, Ashvem Beach, Pernem ■ 0932 610 3486 ■ www.leela cottage.com ■ ₹₹₹
Stay in air-conditioned designer huts, just a stone's throw away from the beach. The interiors are furnished with antiques. A beachfront restaurant and rustic vegan café are on site.

Inland Retreats

Khaama Kethna
MAP D5 ■ 442 Gurawal, Agonda, Canacona ■ 0832 264 7958 ■ www.khaama kethna.com ■ ₹
A tranquil eco-village nestled on the hilltops of Agonda, Khaama Kethna features bamboo tree huts and five exclusive deluxe cabanas or lodges, with private terraces, which open onto lush gardens. All huts have outdoor bathrooms. Guests are provided with linen and mosquito nets. There's a yoga and meditation centre and a garden restaurant.

Project Café
MAP J4 ■ Amalia Villa 198, Mazal Waddo, Assagao ■ 0928 438 9271 ■ www. theprojectcafe.in ■ ₹₹
Amalia House is a charming 130-year-old Portuguese mansion that has been refurbished into an experiential design hotel as well as a multi-disciplinary space. There are six rooms and none

are alike. Also, everything from the furniture to the crockery are for sale and can be ordered. There's also a great restaurant on site.

The Inner Temple
MAP K4 ■ House No. 851, near Moira Club, Moira ■ 0950 357 7779 ■ www. theinnertemple.in ■ ₹₹₹
Set in the village of Moira, this gorgeous Portuguese villa has three beautifully designed large bedrooms, Kamini, Champa and Sachchidananda. All of these have calming interiors. There is a spa and private pool. In addition, yoga classes and meditation workshops are also organized.

Wildernest
MAP E1 ■ Off Sankhali, Chorla Ghat, Chorla ■ 0831 420 7954 ■ www. wildernest-goa.com ■ ₹₹₹
A self-styled eco-resort at an altitude of 816 m (2,677 ft), Wildernest has environmentally friendly thatched structures built with acacia wood and other local materials, but have the amenities of a luxury hotel. Guests can enjoy stunning vistas from the infinity pool. The resort has resident guides and organizes hiking and wildlife-spotting expeditions. Wi-Fi is available only in public areas. Minimum two-night stay required.

Hotels Around Goa

Evolve Back Hampi
Kamalapura – PK Halli Rd, Bellary, Hospet ■ 0839 429 4700 ■ www.evolve back.com ■ ₹₹₹
A short drive away from the ruins of Hampi,

this hotel is built to resemble a 14th-century Vijayanagara-era palace. There are 37 regal suites with opulent furnishings, and nine Jal Mahal pool villas. All have private Jacuzzis. The two restaurants offer gourmet continental and Indian cuisine. Amenities include an infinity pool, lounge bar and Ayurvedic spa. There are walking tours to help guests explore Hampi.

Hampi's Boulders
MAP G2 ■ Junas Waddo, Mandrem ■ 0832 224 7219 ■ www.dunesgoa. com ■ ₹₹₹
Along the banks of the Tungabhadra, this eco-resort is over an hour's drive away from Hampi. There are one to three bedroom boulder-shaped stone cottages, some with air conditioning, balconies and river views, but no Wi-Fi. Relax by the natural rock-cut pool and enjoy a South Indian buffet here. Walks and bird-watching tours are offered.

SwaSwara
Om Beach, Gokarna ■ 0956 259 1622 ■ www. cghearth.com ■ ₹₹₹
This beachfront resort has relaxed wooden villas on a hillside overlooking the bay. All have en-suite bathrooms. A yoga hut and Ayurvedic centre are set in the gardens. The library has Wi-Fi. There are vegetarian and seafood restaurants. Boat cruises are also offered. Minimum five-night stay.

For a key to hotel price categories see p114

General Index

Acknowledgments

Author Beverly Smart

Additional Contributor Meenakshi Sharma

Publishing Director Georgina Dee

Design Director Maxine Pedliham

Delhi Team Head Malavika Talukder

Editorial Parnika Bagla, Dipika Dasgupta, Rachel Fox, Shikha Kulkarni, Anuroop Sanwalia

Cover Design Maxine Pedliham, Bess Daly, Vinita Venugopal

Design Bandana Paul, Priyanka Thakur, Stuti Tiwari Bhatia, Vaishali Vashisht, Vinita Venugopal

Picture Research Sumita Khatwani, Susie Peachey

Cartography Hansa Babra, Mohammad Hassan, Suresh Kumar, Casper Morris

DTP Azeem Siddiqui

Production Samantha Cross

Factchecker Shyamant Behal

Proofreader Shikha Kulkarni

Indexer Anuroop Sanwalia

Illustrator Bandana Paul

Picture Credits

Every effort has been made to trace the copyright holders, and we apologize in advance for any unintentional omissions. We would be pleased to insert the appropriate acknowledgments in any subsequent edition of this publication.

The publisher would like to thank the following for their kind permission to reproduce their photographs:

Key: a-above; b-below/bottom; c-centre; f-far; l-left; r-right; t-top

Alamy Stock Photo: Ian Dagnall 100b; Dinodia Photos 3tl, 45br, 72–3, 99bl; Exotica 74tl, 95tl, 97br; Andrey Khrobostov 89bl; Nikreates 96cla; Simon Reddy 98t; Robertharding / Yadid Levy 60bl.

Anantashram: 103bl.

Ashiyana Yoga Retreat Village: 18clb.

Baba Au Rhum: 61cl, 95c.

Nitin Bhat: 52-3.

The Black Sheep Bistro: 79c.

Butterfly Conservatory of Goa: 31cb, 100c.

Sangram Chatterjee: 11tr, 12bl, 13tl, 13crb, 16-7c, 17tl, 20cl, 21crb, 22crb, 27cl, 44tl.

Chim, Goa: 101tr.

Chronicle Vagator: 57cr, 94b.

Club Cubana: 56t.

Dorling Kindersley: Fredrik Arvidsson / Laurence Arvidsson 42t, 42bc.

Dreamstime.com: Aapthamithra 4crb, 70-1b; Allenkayaa 6cla, 11cla, 30br; Alukashenkov 83cla; Sibi Ar 39clb; Swapan Banik 10cla, 16br, 77cl; Florian Blümm 15tr, 66t; Boggy 26br; Natalia Bogutckaia 24cla; Andrei Bortnikau 18-9c; Paul Brighton 58br; Bubbawilliums 97tl; Adrian Constantinescu 67tr; Viktoriya Samir Dixit 70tl; Stefano Ember 12-3c; Euriico 22t; Francocogoli 85c; Girishhc 32bl, 84cla; Denys Hedrovych 7tr; Valerii Iavtushenko 14-5b, 71cr; Jackmalipan 23bl; Joviton 4b, 68cl, 69br; Maxim Karlione 38-9b; Milind Ketkar 2tr, 40-1; Konstik 33tl; Kosmos111 11b, 64-5; Iuliia Kryzhevska 10bl; Manubahuguna 58cl, 59tl; Jose Mathew 15cl, 34cl, 38cr, 39tr, 50cl, 50-1bc, 69tl, 93tl; Mnf1974 66cl; Murger 51tl; Alexander Mychko 59clb; Vishnu Nair 32cr; Kantilal Patel 4cl, 51tr; Marina Pissarova 3tr, 4t, 4cla, 19tl, 104-5; Ondřej Prosický 11cra; Radiokafka 45t, 68b, 75tr; Dmitry Rukhlenko 47t; Saiko3p 10cl, 10crb, 14cla, 20-1c, 24-5b, 30-1c, 46tl, 46cr, 62tl, 81br, 89t; Olena Serditova 48-9b; Snehal Jeevan Pailkar 27b; Nataliia Sokolovska 24crb, 26tl, 36ca, 36b, 37crb; Spvvkr 10tr, 28-9; Evgenii Sudarev 4clb; Suronin 4cra; Aleksandar Todorovic 2tl, 8-9, 11cr, 47br; Victortyakht 55cc; Alex Zarubin 25tl; Oleg Zhukov 31tr, 80cl.

Gallery Gitanjali: 20br.

Getty Images: Lonely Planet Images / Greg Elms 91cl; Moment / Ashit Desai 86-7.

Goa Chitra Museum: 34br.

Deveshi Halder: 76t.

iStockphoto.com: 1970s 81t; Pavel Laputskov 48tl; lena_serditova 1; VasukiRao 84br.

Jungle Book: 33crb.

Nilesh Korgaokar: 34-5c, 59br, 82b.

Literati: 17br.

LPK Waterfront: 57b.

Mario Gallery: 67bl, 78b.

Museum Houses of Goa: 90b.

Museum of Goa: 43tr, 88tl, 90tl.

SUMMIT FREE PUBLIC LIBRARY

Pa...

Peopl...

Photo Division Ministry of Information and Broad...

Prana Café ...

PunchStock ...
Warren 49c...

MAP INCLUDED

Satsanga Retreat: 92clb.

Shishir Dhulla: @chitrakatha.in 35crb.

Mehak Singhal: 31cr.

Splashdown Waterpark: 54b.

Sublime – Goa: 60t.

Sunaparanta, Goa: 23tr, 37tl.

Sundowner: 102cl.

Vaayu Waterman's Village: 18br.

Velha Goa: 63br.

Brian Yardley: 55tr.

Cover images
Front and spine: **iStockphoto.com:** lena_serditova.

Back: **AWL Images:** GARDEL Bertrand tr; **Dreamstime.com:** Mcherevan tl, Spvvkr cla; **iStockphoto.com:** alan64 crb, lena_serditova b.

Pull Out Map Cover
iStoc...

All ot...
For f...
www.d...

| Penguin Random House |

...ted and bound in China

First Edition 2019

...shed in Great Britain by
...ing Kindersley Limited
80 Strand, London WC2R 0RL

Published in the United States by
DK US, 1450 Broadway Suite 801,
New York, NY 10018, USA

Copyright © 2019 Dorling
Kindersley Limited

A Penguin Random House Company

19 20 21 22 10 9 8 7 6 5 4 3 2 1

A CIP catalogue record is available
from the British Library.

A catalogue record for this book is available
from the Library of Congress.

ISSN 1479-344X
ISBN 978-0-2414-0600-7

Summit Free Public Library

NOV 2019

As a guide to abbreviation in visitor information blocks: **Adm** = admission charge; **D** = dinner; **L** = lunch.

MIX
Paper from
responsible sources
FSC www.fsc.org FSC™ C018179